PERSPECTIVES ON VICTIMOLOGY

Volume 11
SAGE RESEARCH PROGRESS SERIES IN CRIMINOLOGY

ABOUT THE SERIES

The SAGE RESEARCH PROGRESS SERIES IN CRIMINOLOGY is intended for those professionals and students in the fields of criminology, criminal justice, and law who are interested in the nature of current research in their fields. Each volume in the series—four to six new titles will be published in each calendar year—focuses on a theme of current and enduring concern; and each volume contains a selection of previously unpublished essays . . . drawing on presentations made at the previous year's Annual Meeting of the American Society of Criminology.

Now in its third year, the series continues with five new volumes, composed of papers presented at the 30th Annual Meeting of the American Society of Criminology, held in Dallas, Texas, November 8-12, 1978. The volumes in the third year of publication include:

- *Biology and Crime*
  edited by C. R. Jeffery
- *Perspectives on Victimology*
  edited by William H. Parsonage
- *Police Work: Strategies and Outcomes in Law Enforcement*
  edited by David M. Petersen
- *Structure, Law, and Power: Essays in the Sociology of Law*
  edited by Paul J. Brantingham and Jack M. Kress
- *Courts and Diversion: Policy and Operations Studies*
  edited by Patricia L. Brantingham and Thomas G. Blomberg

Previously published volumes include *Violent Crime: Historical and Contemporary Issues* (James A. Inciardi and Anne E. Pottieger, eds.), *Law and Sanctions: Theoretical Perspectives* (Marvin D. Krohn and Ronald L. Akers, eds.), *The Evolution of Criminal Justice: A Guide for Practical Criminologists* (John P. Conrad, ed.), *Quantitative Studies in Criminology* (Charles Wellford, ed.), *Discretion and Control* (Margaret Evans, ed.), *Theory in Criminology: Contemporary Views* (Robert F. Meier, ed.), *Juvenile Delinquency: Little Brother Grows Up* (Theodore N. Ferdinand, ed.), *Contemporary Corrections: Social Control and Conflict* (C. Ronald Huff, ed.), and *Criminal Justice Planning and Development* (Alvin W. Cohn, ed.).

Comments and suggestions from our readers about this series are welcome.

SERIES EDITORS:

James A. Inciardi
University of Delaware

C. Ray Jeffery
Florida State University

SAGE RESEARCH PROGRESS SERIES IN CRIMINOLOGY
VOLUME 11

PERSPECTIVES
on VICTIMOLOGY

Edited by WILLIAM H. PARSONAGE

Published in cooperation with the
AMERICAN SOCIETY of CRIMINOLOGY

 **SAGE** Publications   Beverly Hills   London

For information address:

SAGE Publications, Inc.
275 South Beverly Drive
Beverly Hills, California 90212

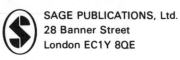

SAGE PUBLICATIONS, Ltd.
28 Banner Street
London EC1Y 8QE

Printed in the United States of America

Library of Congress Cataloging in Publication Data
Main entry under title:

Perspectives on victimology.

(Sage research progress series in criminology; v. 11)
Bibliography: p.
1. Victims of crimes—Addresses, essays, lectures. 2. Victims of crimes—United States—Addresses, essays, lectures. I. Parsonage, William H. II. American Society of Criminology. III. Series.
HV6250.25.P47   362.8'8   79-15524
ISBN 0-8039-1323-0
ISBN 0-8039-1324-9 pbk.

FIRST PRINTING

CONTENTS

William H. Parsonage
Pennsylvania State University

INTRODUCTION

THE VICTIM AS A FOCUS
OF CRIMINOLOGICAL INTEREST

In earlier times, victims of crimes played a significant role in the administration of justice; they, or their kin, took personal responsibility for extracting recompense from the culprits. The period referred to as the "golden age of the victim," beginning with the Middle Ages, was an era when the victim's dominant role was recognized in a range of practices such as the "blood feud," "composition" (the obligation to pay damages), and the intricate "damages and value system" of the Anglo-Saxons (Schafer, 1977).

Then, with the rise of the king and dominance of the state, the rights of the injured were separated from the penal law. Composition emerged as a special field in civil law. From that point, there was an apparent decline in the victim's functional role in crime and criminal law. The only aspect of the criminal-victim relation that continued to be recognized was the harm, injury, or other damages caused by the criminal to his or her victim (Schafer, 1977).

In contrast to the understanding of crime as a violation of the victim's interest, the emergence of the state developed another interpretation: the disturbance of society. As a result, "the unfortunate victim of criminality is habitually ignored." While punishment of crime was regarded as the concern of the state and thus received more and more

AUTHOR'S NOTE: *Special thanks to my friend and colleague Fred W. Vondracek for his assistance in the selection of papers for this book, and to Jennifer Morris for preparing the manuscript.*

7

official and public support, the crime, as a wrong to the victim, came to be regarded as a private matter and from this viewpoint elicited little official or public concern. The state become interested only in the responsibility of the offender; this made the responsibility one-directional [Schafer, 1977: 22].

Recently, there has emerged a renewed recognition of the victim's role in crime. This revival of the victim has been equated with the shift from the "individualistic" to the "universalistic" orientation of criminal law and criminology; that is, from a stiff, static, formalistic, orientation which takes only a narrow view of the crime, to a concern with the criminal's and victim's functional responsibility as participants (Schafer: 1977). The reacknowledgement of the fact that someone indeed has suffered as the result of the commission of a crime has been expressed in two important ways: eligibility for compensation or restitution for his injury or loss at the hands of the offender; and a heightened sensitivity to the need to include the victim in the universe of factors and actors which must be examined in attempts to more fully comprehend the dynamics of crime.

Clear evidence of the revival of the victim's role in crime may be identified by the attention given this topic by the scholarly community of criminologists. Indeed, at the 1978 meetings of the American Society of Criminology in Dallas, Texas, more than thirty papers were presented on victimological issues. Viewed collectively, the concerns reflected in these papers clustered around three general themes: (1) concerns about the development of reliable crime and victimization data and the methodology to secure it; (2) attention to the characteristics of special types of offenders and victims; and (3) interest in assessing and developing strategies to deal with some of the social and personal effects of crime and victimization.

The purpose of this introductory chapter is to establish a foundation and to provide a context to present ten essays selected from more than thirty presented at the 1978 ASC meetings. The essays elaborate the themes mentioned above. While they do not represent the entire range of issues of concern to victimologists, they do address questions which are of great interest to the scholar as well as the professional in the field.

VICTIMOLOGY: AN OVERVIEW

Perhaps the most direct and useful way to begin this discussion of victimology and key victimological issues, is to consider some fundamental questions: (1) What is victimology? (2) What are the kinds of questions it seeks to explore and answer? (3) What are the approaches commonly used in pursuing these objectives? (4) What are some of the practical or potentially practical applications of victimological findings for the society?

Defining Victimology

Victimology has been variously defined as "the study of the criminal-victim relationship" (Schafer, 1977: 1), and as "that branch of criminology which primarily studies the victims of crime and everything that is connected with such a victim" (Drapkin and Viano, 1974: 2). Although there has been concern with criminal-victim relations throughout history, victimology as an identifiable branch of criminology has been traced to the work of Von Hentig in the 1940s. As part of the discipline of criminology, victimology concerns the interaction in which both the criminal offender (the usual target of inquiry) and the victim have functional roles and responsibilities.

Given the broad nature of the field of criminology, it is not unexpected that victimology has been criticized for being narrow. For example, it is charged that victimology explores only a limited range of crimes in the criminal-victim relationship. As Quinney (1972: 316) has said, "Following the positivistic assumptions of causation, criminologists have invested the role of the victim in the commission of offenses. For the most part, however, the criminal-victim relationship has been limited to a narrow range of crimes—primarily murder, aggravated assault, forcible rape and robbery." Indeed, victimology has been reluctant to take into account criminal activity in which society, rather than an identifiable individual, is the victim of crime. So called "victimless crime" begs victimological inquiry.

Foci of Victimological Inquiry

There are several kinds of questions interesting to victimologists. Basically, victimologists have attempted to learn more about the actual extent and nature of crime. There is general agreement that not all crime is known or reported to the police. Several authoritative sources have suggested that if all the categories of offense are considered, it is probably accurate to suggest that most of the behavior that could be classified as violations of the criminal law is not reported to the police. Thus the development of knowledge about the actual frequency or volume of crime, and the factors that influence victims' decisions to report or not to report crime to police, is of obvious significance.

Another interest concerns the question of the relative risk of being victimized. As a matter of conventional wisdom, it is known that certain crime patterns exist and that the prospect of becoming a victim is enhanced by certain factors, and that these factors vary with the type of offense. For example, the prospect of being a victim of rape is influenced, obviously, by one's sex, as well as availability and vulnerability to the sexual offender. But surprisingly, beyond certain fairly gross relationships, there is much to learn about victimization patterns and the economic, ecological, situational, and personal factors that influence them. Associated with the question of relative risk is the more specific question of victim participation in that crime. To what extent do victim attributes precipitate, or otherwise influence, the commission of personal crime? Recognizing that crime is an interactional process which involves to some extent, and in different ways, both the criminal offender and the victim, the systematic development of knowledge about this relation is of considerable import.

Victimologists are also interested in knowing about the kinds and extent of losses, injuries, and damages experienced by victims of crime. Interestingly, there is precious little known about the effects of victimization on individuals and segments of the society apart from knowledge about economic losses. Learning more about other costs, such as the extent of physical injury, psychological, social and interpersonal consequences for the functioning of victims, and the costs associated with the delivery of victims' services, is critical to an understanding of crime.

It should be apparent that the offender has more than a passive role in the criminal-victim relation. Thus, another area of considerable interest is the study of the attributes of offenders and the process by which they make decisions about their involvement in committing a crime. Of particular interest is developing knowledge about what influences the offender's choices in selecting victims, and the extent to which the decision is rational and can, therefore, be influenced. This is perhaps one area where victimologists can ally themselves with more traditional criminological inquiry.

A final concern that must be mentioned has to do with the behavior of the social group—the family and society—toward victims of crime. Just as there are social consequences of being convicted for the commission of crimes, there are consequences of being the victim. Furthermore, victimization results in losses which often require social assistance. The responsiveness of society in meeting these needs, then, is an area of significant interest and increasing inquiry.

Approaches in Victimological Inquiry

There are several methodologies which are frequently used in victimological inquiry. For our purposes, five general approaches will be identified briefly and then discussed. They are: (1) analysis of official crime statistics; (2) victimization surveys; (3) self-report surveys; (4) case studies; and (5) the development of victim typologies.

The *Uniform Crime Report*, a major source of information about crime officially reported, is designed to indicate the extent of reported crimes and certain crime attributes. The *Uniform Crime Report* (UCR) has been published since 1930 and reports statistics on crime known to police. The information has been voluntarily submitted by law enforcement agencies across the country and, despite some important limitations, the UCR is recognized as the most authoritative available source of information on the frequency and distribution of crime in the United States (Vetter and Silverman, 1978). Such data have been heavily used in what is popularly called "epidemiological" studies of crime: crime rates that have been examined in relation to demography and other factors. Vetter and Silverman point out a number of limitations concerning the development and use of UCR data:

1) the difficulty of determining the true volume of crime; 2) the fact that statistics are not compiled for all offenses; 3) the emphasis on percent changes in the total volume of index offenses; 4) the practice of defining a crime as cleared when a suspect has been charged, regardless of the verdict; 5) the failure to base crime rates without taking into account the relative seriousness of the crime; 7) the inability to relate statistics to various phases of the criminal justice process; 8) the differential enforcement of criminal statutes; 9) the failure to devise a system that would take into consideration "accommodations which distort present figures"; and 10) the voluntary nature of primary data collection [1978: 33].

In spite of all these limitations, it is important to point out that the UCR is the only compilation of crime statistics on a nationwide basis and it represents an important source of information for victimological research.

A second approach used in victimological studies is the victimization survey. The National Crime Survey (NCS) is the major victimization survey and is designed to produce time series data on crime, to show how personal, household, business, and environmental characteristics are related to the chances of being victimized, to estimate the consequences of crime, and to describe characteristics related to official crime reporting. Thus, the special contribution of the NCS in victimological inquiry is significant and obvious. It provides an index of victim attributes which is of extreme relevance in the exploration of the victim-criminal relationship. And it yields important information about the losses incurred by victims of crimes. It must be said, however, that victimization surveys are not without their liabilities. Levine (1976) has cautioned against placing undue faith in victimization surveys. Proponents have sometimes failed to recognize problems of validity caused by false reporting by respondents (e.g., mistaken interpretation and classification of incidents as crime, memory failure about when crimes occurred, lying) and interviewer biases, as well as problems with coding reliability. Even with these limitations, victimization surveys contribute significantly to the achievement of the following goals: (1) furnishing a means for developing victim typologies; (2) providing data for computing relative risk of victimization for certain segments of the population; (3) assisting in the determination of the costs and effects of crime; and (4) providing greater understanding of why certain crimes are not reported to the police (Vetter and Silverman, 1978: 352).

A third approach is the use of the Self-Report Survey. Briefly, self-report surveys are used to assess hidden crime and, further, to secure information about the attributes of offenders as well as their motivation and methods in the conduct of offenses. Most commonly, such research uses printed survey instruments to be completed and returned by the respondent. Adaptations of this are the anonymous telephone interview, or the face-to-face interview. As with the other approaches used in generating information concerning victimology, these methods have some limitations that must be understood. A principal limitation is the possibility of concealment by the respondent. Likewise, self-reports suffer from the same kinds of validity problems as does the victimization survey discussed earlier.

The Case Study is a fourth method. Very often case studies concern special categories of offenders or victims. For example, intensive investigation is conducted concerning the backgrounds, offenses, and current functioning of offenders who have been convicted of specific offenses.

Similar inquiries are conducted with groups who have been the victims of specific types of crimes. The value of the case study approach is the opportunity it affords for viewing and examining individual behavior in a developmental context. Yet, as in the case of other approaches, its limitations must be recognized. For example, a primary problem is the limited ability to generalize to larger segments of the population.

The fifth and final approach to be discussed is the victim typology. Victim typologies aid in achieving a clearer understanding of the victim's role in the causation of the criminal offenses, and in the development of measures for treating victims of crime, including compensation and restitution programs (Vetter and Silverman, 1978: 342). For example, the victim's participation in the offense may range from very active to passive. Von Hentig classified victims according to a scheme of relative weakness or vulnerability. Mendelsohn's typology used their amount of guilt vis-à-vis the criminal in the conduct of the offense. Other typologies such as those developed by Fattah, classify the interaction between victims and criminals by social and psychological traits. The problems in using typologies are the same as those experienced in any endeavor that attempts to classify; they are limitations in the ability to be comprehensive, muttually exclusive, empirically verifiable, and to possess clarity and objectivity. The Sellin-Wolfgang typology, which more clearly deals with the measurable attributes of the offender-victim interaction, goes farther than other typologies in meeting the criteria identified above (Silverman, 1977).

The Utility of Victimology

It is reasonable to expect that victimological research should have practical and socially useful applications for predicting, preventing, and for dealing with the effects of crime. One application stems from its attempt to ascertain the extent and nature of crime. Victim surveys have shown that the actual crime rate is probably twice as high as that reported by the *Uniform Crime Report*. Data from victim surveys provide an alternative to the UCR: one can obtain a different sense of increases in crime rates as well as a means to estimate police effectiveness.

Another useful application of victim survey research is the light that it sheds on the disparity between actual and reported crime rates by identifying what influences victims' decisions to report or not report (Glaser, 1974). For example, victim surveys reveal that the victim's attitude toward the police is a primary intervening variable in the decision to report or not to report a crime. Research in victimology indicates a relation between perceived police effectiveness and the propensity to report crime. If police are viewed as being effective in solving crimes, report rates rise; if there is a perception of ineffectiveness, report rates fall. Another factor found to influence reporting rates is the victim's view of personal consequences likely to follow such action. Forcible rape is probably the most underreported major crime—and for several reasons. They include the potential for publicity, the fear of rape victims being interrogated by the police, the ordeal of questioning and physical examination by medical authorities, the testimony in open court, and the trauma of facing their attackers. The value of this knowledge is obvious in developing new procedures for handling rape victims: Care must be taken to be sensitive to their fears and needs, and to provide support and the assistance necessary to help them through the ordeal. Moreover, to the extent that these matters can be addressed, the likelihood of successful prosecution of rapists is enhanced.

Obtaining information concerning the relative risk of crime victimization among special segments of the population has valuable consequences for the creation of various preventive and remedial programs. Even though elderly citizens are less likely to be victimized than young males, senior citizens manifest considerable fear about crime victimization. They are often physically ill or weak, unable to take care of property, and depend on others for assistance. These weaknesses make them especially vulnerable to fraudulent crime. Research in victimology has created programs to educate senior citizens. Knowledge of various house repair schemes, and so forth, have saved innumerable citizens from being victimized by fraud.

Victimization information has also stimulated restitution and victim compensation programs. Knowledge of the extreme financial losses incurred by victims of crime has increased the tendency of courts and correctional authorities to order and otherwise encourage restitution by offenders. An interesting example of a special restitution program is that run by the Minnesota Department of Corrections (1976). Specially selected property offenders are released from prison to live at Restitution House, a community-based center. A contract is made between the offender, his victim, and the Department of Corrections; the offender then works in the community and pays restitution as well as room and board at the facility. This type of program is an interesting innovation because it relates to the criminal-victim relationship.

While the notion of forcing the offender to pay the victim for losses is a sensible and popular one as a general program, it has many limitations and liabilities. Victimological inquiry has revealed the following: (1) Only a minority of offenders are convicted and are, therefore, available for court ordered restitution; (2) Offenders usually have few resources or assets which would provide a basis for repayment; (3) Prison earnings of convicted offenders are insignificant to cover restitution; (4) The likely cost to the state administering a comprehensive offender restitution program is likely to exceed the money received by victims (MacNamara and Sullivan, 1974): 1974: 233).

In an attempt to develop an alternative approach to reduce the victim's losses, several states have passed victims' compensation statutes. Evaluating the operation of these programs has revealed that there are a number of problems with such legislation and its effective implementation.

Among the major difficulties encountered have been:

fraudulent claims and attempts at multiple recoveries; questionable awards in some cases, which violate either the statute itself or the criteria for eligibility; inflated bills for medical expenses submitted by physicians, hospitals, and

pharmacies; the failure of those who have submitted applications for compensation to receive any awards; and the
tendency in nearly all jurisdictions for bureaucratic red tape
and long delays to discourage applicants [Vetter and Silverman, 1978: 374].

Several suggestions have been forthcoming which criminologists hope would overcome some of these difficulties.
For example, there have been proposals for victims' insurance schemes on the order of unemployment compensation.
Fooner (1974) has raised some cautions about victims compensation legislation to the extent that such programs might
contribute to a temptation/opportunity pattern.

Another example of the application of victimology concerns the sentencing of criminal offenders. Currently, new
sentencing statutes have been enacted in a number of
states which, among other things, are intended to reduce
unreasonable sentencing disparity. Presumptive sentencing
schemes have been, and will continue to be, dependent on
assessments of the relative participation and responsibility
of victims and criminals in the offense, as well as other
offender and victim characteristics. Again, victimological
research has important applications for social policy and
individual administration of the law.

A final application to be mentioned briefly is the value
of victimological research in the development and evaluation of victims' service delivery programs. Dussich (1975)
has conducted extremely interesting and useful analyses of
various victims' services programs. The value of any program is, as he says, its ability to deliver victim restoration
services and contribute to crime reduction. Obviously,
information concerning the variety of losses incurred by
victims of crimes, and the relative risk of victimization
have important application for the development of programs
to deliver the kinds of services Dussich recommends.

ORGANIZATION OF THE BOOK

The forgoing discussion has, it is hoped, provided a context within which to present, and appreciate, the contribu-

tions of colleagues whose ten papers compose the rest of this book. For the purposes of this volume, the essays have been organized around three integrative themes:

  I. Victimization Data: Developing A Basis For Empirical Inquiry
 II. Illustrative Studies: Special Groups of Victims and Offenders
III. Responses To Victimization

Section I features two essays, each of which concerns methodological issues. In the lead article, James Nelson deals with the question of whether the UCR and the NCS crime measures are highly related. The answer to this question is of considerable significance in that inferences made on the basis of comparing the UCR and NCS are legitimate only if it is known to what extent they are measuring the same crimes.

Professors Edna Erez and Simon Hakim use an economic approach in the second article. They apply utility maximization theory of consumer behavior in an analysis that seeks to explain crime as a rational process based on the concept of profitability. Economic motivation and spatial distribution of crime are examined in a manner that yields useful information for prevention, planning, and coordination of law enforcement efforts.

Section II is composed of five interesting studies. The first article by Carl Pope, uses National Crime Survey victimization data to study the relationship between household victimization and neighborhood characteristics. In particular, specific population characteristics are linked to crime rates in an attempt to develop an ecological linkage between victims and offenders.

In a second essay, William Berg and Robert Johnson look at the processes by which the elderly and females acquiesce to the role of victim. Part of the discussion analyzes the factors which influence the vulnerability of different population groups to embracing the victim role.

Vernetta Young et al. compare the characteristics of the victims of female offenders with those of victims of male offenders, using National Crime Survey data. The essay particularly elucidates the victim-offender relationship, which she finds to be sufficiently different for women offenders than for male offenders to warrant further study.

Decker, O'Brien and Shichor examine urban structural characteristics such as population density, racial composition, and so forth, and the victimization of juveniles. This article is of particular interest because it deals with the urban juvenile as victim rather than as offender.

Samuel Smithyman's article is the fifth featured in this section. It is his contention that there is a problem in the way information about rape and the characteristics of offenders and victims has been developed. This interesting study analyzes information gained from anonymous telephone interviews with persons representing themselves as rapists. Among the most startling findings of this study, the author reports that more than three-fourths of the "rapists" had no criminal records, and that as a group they represented the socioeconomic spectrum from lower to upper middle class.

The final section, Section III, emphasizes the responses of victims of crimes, and the implications for their adjustment. John Hepburn and Daniel Monti use multivariate analyses to ascertain the relations between school related victimization, fear of crime, and adaptive responses among high school students who are victimized.

Marx Blumberg explores the relations among injury and victim characteristics, offender characteristics, and situational characteristics. Of particular interest is an analysis of the effects of weapons possession by offenders and the employment of self-protective measures by victims.

Finally, Veronen, Kilpatrick, and Resick present a model of fear and the conditioning framework which explains development of fears and phobias in victims of rape. They describe their research of responses to rape and then present findings which have applicability to criminal justice personnel in dealing with rape victims.

As the forgoing descriptions of the contributing authors' essays suggest, this book addresses a range of victimological issues which have practical as well as academic applications. The "mix" of concerns and approaches reflected truly provides interesting "Perspectives on Victimology."

REFERENCES

DRAPKIN, I. and E. VIANO [eds.] (1974) Victimology. Lexington: D. C. Heath.

DUSSICH, J.P.J. (1975) "Victim service models and the efficacy." Presented to the International Advanced Study Institute on Victimology and the Needs of Contemporary Society, Bellagio, Italy.

FOONER, M. (1974) "Victim-induced, victim-invited, and victim-precipitated criminality: some problems in evaluation of proposals for victim compensation," pp. 231-233 in I. Drapkin and E. Viano (eds.) Victimology. Lexington: D. C. Heath.

GLASER, D. (1970) "Victim survey research: theoretical implications," in A. L. Guenther (ed.) Criminal Behavior and Social Systems. New York: Harper & Row.

LEVINE, J. P. (1976) "The potential for crime overreporting in criminal victimization surveys." Criminology 3: 307-330.

MacNAMARA, D.E.J. and J. J. SULLIVAN (1974) "Composition, restitution, compensation: making the victim whole," in I. Drapkin and E. Viano (eds.) Victimology. Lexington: D. C. Heath.

Minnesota Department of Corrections (1976) "The Minnesota restitution center." Minneapolis: State of Minnesota.

QUINNEY, R. (1972) "Who is the victim?" Criminology 3: 314-323.

SCHAFER, S. (1977) Victimology: The Victim and His Criminal. Reston, VA: Reston Publishing.

SILVERMAN, R. A. (1974) "Victim typologies: overview, critique, and reformulation," pp. 55-65 in I. Drapkin and E. Viano (eds.) Victimology. Lexington: D. C. Heath.

VETTER, H. J. and I. J. SILVERMAN (1978) The Nature of Crime. Philadelphia: W. B. Saunders.

James F. Nelson
SUNY, Albany

1

IMPLICATIONS FOR
THE ECOLOGICAL STUDY OF CRIME
A Research Note

INTRODUCTION

The estimation of crime rates has been and continues to be based largely on the *Uniform Crime Report* (UCR). The validity of this measure has frequently been questioned largely because only officially reported crimes are counted, and because the recording of these crimes may vary from police precinct to precinct. In the late 1960s and early 1970s, a second major method of measuring crime, called the National Crime Survey (NCS), was developed by the Law Enforcement Assistance Administration (LEAA). The NCS was instituted to obtain a stable measurement of crime that could show relationships between crime incidents and victim characteristics in different areas and across time. It is more ambitious than the UCR in that details of criminal victimizations are recorded regardless of whether or not the crime was reported to the police. It is less ambitious in that fewer crimes are studied, and random samples of households and businesses in selected areas are interviewed. In contrast, the UCR tries to record the crimes experienced by all households, persons, and businesses.

AUTHOR'S NOTE: *This article is abstracted from a paper entitled, "Alternative Measures of Crime: A Comparison of the Uniform Crime Report and the National Crime Survey in 26 American Cities," presented at the 1978 meetings of the American Society of Criminology, Dallas. The author would like to thank Betsy Colvin, Michael Gottfredson, and Michael Hindelang for helpful comments.*

The question raised here is are NCS and UCR crime measures highly related to each other? If they are, then the often criticized UCR would be supported as a legitimate measure of crime to the extent that NCS is a legitimate measure of crime. But if they are not, the validity of measuring the level of crime of either or both the UCR and the NCS rates would be uncertain.

The relation of UCR and NCS crime rates was estimated by first calculating NCS crime specific rates in twenty-six American cities to be definitionally as similar to UCR rates as possible, and then by measuring the correlation between the rates for each type of crime. This procedure was preferred to comparing differences in rates because the magnitude of rates is likely to depend both on differences in design of the measures, and on methodological shortcomings. These differences will be briefly reviewed before the correlations are presented. A fuller account of the analysis is presented in Nelson (forthcoming).

DIFFERENCES BETWEEN
UCR AND NCS CITY SAMPLES

The most obvious difference between the NCS city samples and the UCR data is that the NCS was based on random samples of households and businesses within selected cities, whereas the UCR was based on persons who reported crimes to the police within each city. (A complete description of the NCS may be found in Garofalo and Hindelang, 1977.) This immediately suggests that NCS rates should be higher than UCR rates because not all persons reported crimes to the police. The NCS data support this suggestion. About two-thirds of the simple assaults, about one-half of the personal robberies, rapes, aggravated assaults and household burglaries, and about one-fourth of the motor vehicle thefts reported to the NCS interviewers were not reported to the police (these figures varied somewhat by city).

If respondents reported all victimizations to the NCS interviewers, then NCS rates could be made more similar to UCR rates by basing NCS rates only on crimes the respondent said were reported to the police. Unfortunately, not all victimizations were reported to the NCS interviewers. Using a relatively small sample, the San Jose Methods Test of Known Crime Victims (LEAA, 1972) showed that over half of the assaults, about one-third of the rapes, about one-fourth of the robberies, and about one-tenth of the burglaries previously reported to the police were not reported to NCS interviewers. This suggests that victimizations involving theft were more likely to be reported to NCS interviewers than were personal victimizations without theft.

The NCS city rates are also expected to differ from UCR rates because of memory problems involving (1) the recollection of each victimization; and (2) the details of each incident. The first of these problems is affected by whether interviews are bounded. Interviews are bounded when respondents are surveyed about the victimizations they experienced since the last interview. They are unbounded when respondents are interviewed only once. Murphy and Cowan (1976) demonstrated that the number of victimizations reported at a second interview tended to be less than the number reported for a comparable period before the first interview. Apparently, respondents recall victimizations that occur before the reference period as if they had occurred within the reference period more often with unbounded than with bounded interviews. This suggests that the city rates may be inflated because unbounded interviews were used.

NCS rates may also differ from UCR rates because persons frequently forgot details of related victimizations. If a respondent experienced at least three similar victimizations, and was unable to recall the details of each separate victimization, then these incidents were recorded as a series victimization, and details of only the last victimization were recorded. This makes it impossible to know exactly how many incidents of which type occurred. Most reports based on the NCS data have eliminated these victimizations from rate calculations. The data reported by

Shenk and McInery (1978) may be used to show that omitting series victimizations from rate calculations may deflate the number of assault and rape victimizations by 30 to 40%, the number of robbery and burglary victimizations by 15 to 20% and the number of motor vehicle thefts by 3 to 4%. Similar results are reported by Hindelang (1976).

Even if NCS respondents accurately remembered all victimizations and reported them to the NCS interviewers, the NCS and UCR rates would likely differ because of different populations included in each data set. First, the NCS was based on persons aged twelve and over who lived within city boundaries. City rates are usually calculated so that crimes occurring to its residents both inside and outside the city are counted with each city's crimes. For example, a crime that occurred to a resident of St. Louis while on vacation in New York City would be tabulated with crimes for St. Louis. This problem was noted by LEAA in its preface to NCS reports as one of the reasons UCR and NCS rates should not be compared. The difference is not likely to severely affect rates, however. Garofalo (1977) showed that nearly 95% of all personal victimizations reported in the NCS city data occurred to residents within their own city. Furthermore, the argument that rates may differ because the NCS is based on a different age group (namely persons twelve and over), whereas the UCR is based upon all persons, is not likely to affect rates very much because the majority of crimes reported to the police occur to persons age twelve and over.

Perhaps the most significant difference between populations covered in both reports was that persons living outside a city's boundaries could affect UCR rates by being victimized within the city, but they could not affect NCS residentially based crime rates. This bias was partially compensated for by adjusting the population base for the UCR rates in each city by the number of workers who migrated into and out of the city on a daily basis. Since more persons migrated into than out of each city, the bases for all rate calculations were somewhat larger for UCR than for NCS data.

RELATION OF UCR AND NCS RATES

Seven types of crime reports in the NCS were compatible with crimes reported in the UCR. The number of aggravated assaults, simple assaults, motor vehicle thefts, and rapes were estimated by the same definitions in both reports. The NCS data for armed and unarmed robbery were combined for personal and commercial surveys to match the UCR definitions. Similarly, the household and commercial burglaries were combined to correspond to the UCR burglary data. Crime specific rates were estimated by dividing the number of each type of crime (which were weighted in the NCS samples to reflect population sizes) by the population exposed to each crime. For all but burglary, the exposed population equalled the city population for NCS rates, and the residential population adjusted for daily migration of workers for the UCR rates. For burglary, the estimated number of households were used as the population base for both rates.

The linear relations between UCR and NCS rates are summarized in Table 1. The table shows that UCR and NCS rates were: strongly related for motor vehicle theft and robbery with a weapon; moderately related for burglary; weakly related for robbery without a weapon; and were independent, or even negatively related, for aggravated assault, simple assault, and rape. The NCS rates were recaluclated several ways to learn if the weak relationship could be due to differences in reporting crimes to the police, due to excluding series victimizations, or due to differences in seriousness of the assault crimes. When the NCS rates were based only on persons who said they reported the crime to the police, the correlation between UCR and NCS unarmed robbery increased from .56 to .69, but the other correlations remained largely unchanged. The relation between UCR and NCS rates did not increase when assault and rape victimizations were based upon the total number of series and the estimated number of nonseries victimizations. The correlation of assault charges did not increase when NCS assaults were based only on assault victims who received an injury.

TABLE 1

Percentage of Variance Explained and Zero-Order Correlations
Between UCR[a] and NCS[b] Crime Rates

Crime	Variance explained and zero-order correlation	
Motor vehicle theft	82%	(r = .91)
Robbery with a weapon	65	(r = .81)
Burglary	47	(r = .69)
Robbery without a weapon	31	(r = .56)
Simple assault	0	(r = .05)
Rape	0	(r = .04)
Aggravated assault	13	(r = −.36)

a. Source: Unpublished data supplied by the Uniform Crime Reporting section of the FBI.
b. Source: Analysis of data tapes supplied by the Bureau of the Census.

DISCUSSION AND IMPLICATIONS

In general, NCS rates were moderately to strongly related to UCR rates for victimizations characterized by theft, but were unrelated or even negatively related for personal victimizations not characterized by theft. The correlations between UCR and NCS rates for auto theft and armed robbery were sufficiently strong to expect ecological studies of city crime to arrive at the same basic conclusions using either UCR or NCS data. The correlations for burglary and unarmed robbery were lower, suggesting that some differences could be expected depending on whether UCR or NCS rates were used. The correlations for simple assault, aggravated assault, and rape were so low that ecological correlates of one of these rates may *not* provide information about ecological correlates of the other.

The lack of a relation between UCR and NCS personal crimes without theft is quite disturbing. It suggests that conclusions about ecological correlates of personal crime may be methodological artifacts. It is not clear which measure of crime, the UCR or the NCS, is closer to a true or ideal measure of personal crime. They appear to be measuring different things.

In contrast, the high correlation between crimes of theft suggests that inferences about ecological correlates can be made from either UCR or NCR rates. (This conclusion is based on the admittedly tenuous assumption that the two crime rates do not share a common bias—e.g., crimes with a loss are more likely to be reported to both the police and the NCS interviewers.) Because UCR rates exist for nearly every city in the United States, whereas only twenty-six cities were included in the NCS city data, it appears that the UCR data should be used to analyze the ecological correlates of theft crimes. In general, the close correspondence of theft rates between NCS and UCR data adds validity to the use of the UCR data as a measure of the relative number of theft crimes.

The independence of UCR and NCS assault and rape rates may be due to the vagueness and embarrassment associated with these crimes. The NCS data showed that these crimes had the lowest percentages of incidents said to have been reported to the police of all crimes studied in this paper. Not only were these crimes underreported to the police, but rape and assault were underreported to NCS interviewers more than other crimes. Perhaps vehicle theft, burglary, and robbery were well reported to police agencies because these crimes frequently involved expensive property, are covered by insurance, or are not likely to be victim precipitated. In contrast, rape and assault crimes do not usually involve significant theft losses, are not covered by insurance, and may be victim precipitated. For example, it is sometimes difficult to distinguish the victim from the offender in assault cases.

The strong positive correlations between UCR and NCS theft crime rates do not necessarily mean that the detailed data about individuals available in the NCS provide information about which individuals are victimized in UCR reports, nor do the weak correlations between UCR and NCS personal crime rates without theft necessarily mean that the detailed data about individuals in the NCS do not provide information about which individuals are victimized in UCR reports. The present study has only shown that ecological correlations between UCR and NCS crime rates at the city level of analysis are more similar for theft than for personal crimes without theft. The ecological correlations suggest that the individual correlates of the chances of being victimized for NCS and UCR type of data are likely to be more similar for theft than for personal crimes without theft. This is not a mathematical necessity, though. Furthermore, this inference cannot be easily tested until more information on the individual characteristics of crime victims are published in the UCR.

REFERENCES

GAROFALO, J. (1977) "Local victim surveys: a review of the issues." Analytic Report SVAD2. Law Enforcement Assistance Administration, National Criminal Justice Information and Statistics Service. Washington, DC: Government Printing Office.

——— and M. HINDELANG (1977) "An introduction to the National Crime Survey." Analytic Report SVAD4. Law Enforcement Assistance Administration, National Criminal Justice Information and Statistics Service. Washington, DC: Government Printing Office.

HINDELANG, M. J. (1976) Criminal Victimization in Eight American Cities. Cambridge, MA: Ballinger.

Law Enforcement Assistance Administration (1972) San Jose Methods Test of Known Crime Victims. Statistics Technical Report No. 1. Washington, DC: Government Printing Office.

MURPHY, L. R. and C. D. COWAN (1976) "Effects of bounding on telescoping in the National Crime Survey." U.S. Bureau of the Census. Presented at the American Statistical Association Meetings, August 23-26, Boston.

NELSON, J. F. (forthcoming) "Alternative measures of crime: a comparison of the Uniform Crime Report and the National Crime Survey in 26 American cities," in D. Georges and K. Harries (eds.) Crime: A Spatial Perspective. New York: Columbia Univ. Press.

SHENK, F. and W. McINERNEY (1978) "Issues arising from applications of the National Crime Survey." U.S. Bureau of the Census. Presented at the 1978 Annual Meeting of the Southwestern Political Science Association, Houston.

Edna Erez
University of Baltimore

Simon Hakim
Temple University

2

A GEO-ECONOMIC APPROACH TO THE
DISTRIBUTION OF CRIMES IN
METROPOLITAN AREAS

The study of suburban crime has been generally neglected by criminologists because until recently most crime was concentrated in large urban centers. However, the distinctions between city and suburban crime rates appear to be decreasing each year, particularly for property crimes. The reasons are that suburban populations have been growing enormously, and the conditions of big cities have spread to the suburbs (e.g., commercial activities, anonymity). Even in the traditional high middle class suburbs, various property crime rates have been approaching those of the big cities. In part, this change can be attributed to the increased mobility which automobiles and improved highways have given criminals from the city, and in part to the delinquency of suburban juveniles.

The present paper examines the spatial distribution of property crimes in suburban communities and attempts to relate the crime level to various attributes of these communities.

Using economics to explain criminal behavior has recently gained attention in the criminological literature (Ehrlich, 1972; Chapman, 1976; Palmer, 1977). These articles base their theoretical discussions on Becker's innovative paper

AUTHORS' NOTE: *The authors wish to thank Dr. Marvin E. Wolfgang for his valuable comments and suggestions.*

(1968) where the utility maximization theory of consumer behavior in microeconomics is used to explain the conditions inducing an individual to commit a crime. This approach assumes that an offender commits an offense if the expected pecuniary income, as well as the nonpecuniary gratification generated by the act, are greater than the expected costs. Costs are viewed as those directly involved in planning and implementing the crime, and the expected loss due to the punishment and the psychic costs of committing a criminal act. Moreover, a person will commit an offense if his expected utility exceeds that which can be gained by engaging his time and resources in alternative legal activities. In short, the economic approach argues that the commission of an offense is related to the expected legal and illegal income, the probability of apprehension and conviction, and the costs borne by the offender if punished.

Although this approach has been used to explain both property and violent criminal behavior, its application to the analysis of property crime is more straightforward. Therefore, the following analysis is restricted to the spatial distribution of property offenses in suburban communities.

BACKGROUND

Spatial aspects of crime patterns have been well documented by sociologists and criminologists, the major work being that of the "ecological school." In this tradition, the location of offenders is explained by the social, economic, and cultural attributes of neighborhoods where the offenders reside; or, alternatively, crime is explained by elements of the area where the crime is committed. Only a few studies have attempted to tie these two elements to an integrated process of criminal activity, namely, to analyze the relation between the residence of the offender and the area where the crime is committed.

Various studies have analyzed the elements of residential areas which may predispose its inhabitants to criminal behavior. These elements have been labelled variously as "social disorganization" (Shaw and McKay, 1942; Schmid, 1960); "anomie" (Bordua, 1958), and socioeconomic conditions (Quinney, 1964; Beasley and Antunes 1974). The location of crimes has gained less attention in ecological studies. Factors associated with crime areas have been conceptualized as environmental opportunities for specific crimes (Boggs, 1965). The least developed are studies of travel patterns of criminals in their movement from residence to crime site. These studies generally emphasize orientation to the Central Business District (DeFleur, 1967), high income residential areas (Pyle, et al., 1974; Boggs, 1965), or identifying factors that influence the distance offenders travel to commit crime (Boggs, 1965; Rengert, 1977). These studies point out that for property offenses *profitability* has the effect of increasing the distance between offender's residence and the crime site, and that *accessibility* influences the choice between alternative opportunities.

An economic approach includes, in addition to these determinants, the opportunity costs involved in implementing the crime, i.e., the probability of apprehension and punishment. We therefore, consider the effectiveness of police to be a major factor in the decision to commit an offense. The effect of intensified police activity on crime, particularly property offenses, has been documented in past research (Rand Corporation, 1971; Chaiken, 1974). The displacement phenomenon following police activity and crime prevention programs—the resultant offenders' mobility in terms of time and place to avoid apprehension—has also been substantiated (Reppetto, 1976), particularly for property offenses (Rand Corporation, 1971; Hunt et al., 1977).

THE STUDY

The spatial distribution of property offenses in the metropolitan area of Philadelphia is examined by considering simultaneously two related issues: (1) factors determining the "export" of crime by certain communities; and (2) determinants of the "import" or attraction of crimes to other communities.

The geo-economic approach seeks to explain which crimes will be committed, and their location once it is assumed that a "pool" of potential criminals generated by psychological and social causes (the ecological approach) exists within a metropolitan area. The number of property crimes actually committed and their distribution within the communities depends on the opportunities which arise and the costs involved. These opportunities vary among the communities or neighborhoods in the metropolitan area.

Over one hundred independent local municipalities which vary in size, police performance, wealth, and concentration of commercial activity, exist in a typical American metropolitan area (S.M.S.A.). The central city usually contains a significant portion of the metropolitan area's unemployed, low income residents, young male population in the 15-24 age group, and minority groups. Although the suburban communities are diverse in their population, land use, and police performance (Mehay, 1977), these communities generally have a relatively high concentration of wealthy residents and shopping malls. Therefore, a potential criminal who wishes to maximize his net benefits from property crime, and who resides within a metropolitan area is faced with several communities which vary in the factors relevant to his decision about where to commit the crime.

Once we confront a potential criminal with several possible locations for committing the crime, each exhibiting a different subjective expected net benefit, we are then dealing with a distribution similar to established migration and trip distribution models (Bruton, 1975: ch. 3-6).

Thus, our aims in this study are threefold: (1) a comparison of the levels of criminality (property offenses, the four categories in the FBI crime index) between our study areas —suburban places and the neighboring cities. It is our hypothesis that absolute and relative differences in attractiveness among adjacent localities produce incentives for offenders' migration to the more attractive targets; (2) an examination of the distribution of crime within the constituent communities of our study vis-à-vis the attributes of the communities which determine the expected costs and benefits of potential offenses, and; (3) a statistical testing of the hypothesized relations in order to ascertain any significant relations of the variables examined in the second part.

We are aware of the fact that we are using data related to crimes rather than criminals and of the risks involved in using such indirect data, i.e., the ecological fallacy (Robinson, 1950). However, property crimes have a very low clearance rate (14% in the study area for the year 1970). Apprehended criminals may constitute a biased sample of the offender population; therefore, data about crimes, aggregated for each community rather than data about criminals are the better source of information for analysis.

THE STUDY AREA

The area selected for study is a suburban subregion which contains ninety-four communities in Southern New Jersey within the Philadelphia metropolitan area: Burlington, Gloucester, and Camden (excluding Camden City) Counties. This area is a general suburban paradigm because it is typical of most of the eastern suburban areas in the U.S. relative to physical and socioeconomic characteristics, as well as crime rates and distributions. The 1970 population of the municipalities range from 1,147 to 64,395; their developed areas range from 0.22 to 57.8 square miles. These communities are mostly suburban, including old and new settlements, as well as some rural areas that have undergone slow suburbanization since 1965.

Property crime levels of these communities have increased between 1967 and 1975 at an annual rate of 17%; police expenditure increased at the same rate. However, the percentage of police expenditure in the total operating budget which is "clear" of inflationary trends, as well as of differences in wealth, have been constant at 25% over the same period. These facts might indicate that decisions about police budgets are little if at all affected by crime increases;

rather, the police expenditure traditionally is kept to a certain proportion of the total municipal budget.

If this fact is confirmed in other empirical studies, then several studies which represent the "state of the art" in attempting to explain and predict crime are incorrect in specifying the variables (e.g., Greenwood et al., 1973; Zipin et al., 1974; McPheters et al., 1974; Carr Hill et al., 1973; Chapman, 1976). In specifying a simultaneous equations system they all incorporate demand crime variable(s) to explain the level of police expenditure, inferring that the more crimes are committed, the more is allocated for police services. But since this assertion might not explain community police budgetary decisions, their estimation of the whole system, including the crime equation, is incorrect.

Comparison of Study Area with Adjacent Large Cities

Comparing the study area (as one suburban unit) to the adjacent regional cities of Camden, Philadelphia, Trenton, and Wilmington, reveals that the suburban unit spends much less on police expenditure (either per capita or per acre), performs less intensive (lower number of police officers per acre) and possibly less effective (lower clearance rate) police services. Property crime opportunities are greater in the study area; consequently, the value of stolen property per property crime is higher (see Table 1).

Crime in the Suburbs (The Study Area) by Classes of Communities

In the previous section we suggested that rational offenders prefer to commit offenses in certain areas: those in which the potential gain is higher and the risks are lower. In this section we examine several reasons for the distribution of crime within the study area. We have classified communities into functional and spatial categories which may provide additional variables to be included in calculating the choice of a crime target.

Places are considered suburban or rural according to the Census Bureau definition (functional categoralization). The

TABLE 1

**Police Expenditure, Manpower, Crime Level and Characteristics of
Municipalities in the Greater Philadelphia Metropolitan Area**

	Study Area	Camden	Philadelphia	Trenton	Wilmington
1. Median value of owner occupied housing	17,000	8,400	10,600	9,400	11,000
2. Number of police officers per acre	0.32	6.03	9.46	6.65	3.28
3. Police expenditure per capita ($)	19.86	39.72	78.61	39.29	42.28
4. Police expenditure per acre ($)	49.29	731.50	1,862.62	856.60	411.67
5. Police expenditure per dollar stolen property ($)	1.30	1.46	6.09	1.57	1.56
6. Percent spent on police services of total budget	26%	23%	26%	21%	11%
7. Percent property recovered of total property stolen	29.5%	58.5%	48.3%	39.8%	58.4%
8. Value of property stolen per property crime ($)	480.12	419.42	613.31	364.55	370.83
9. Property crime per acre	0.0193	1.1979	0.4983	1.4929	0.7104
10. Per capita property crime	0.0197	0.0650	0.0210	0.0685	0.0730

Sources: Federal Bureau of Investigation, 1970 Uniform Crime Reports. N.J. Department of Community Affairs, 1970 Statements of Financial Condition of Counties and Municipalities. U.S. Department of Commerce, 1970 Census of Population. U.S. Department of Commerce, 1970 Census of Housing, vol. 1. Financial Reports of the Cities of Philadelphia and Wilmington.

historical-core includes old communities in the northern part of Camden County along Route 30 which leads from Philadelphia to Atlantic City. These communities are accessible to both Camden and Philadelphia and have always been oriented to Philadelphia (spatial categorization). In Camden County, the cross-classification suburban-accessible comprises communities especially attractive to offenders due to accessibility, wealth, and commercial establishments (functional and spatial categorization).

Table 2 compares the standardized values (by developed areas) of the three most important interacting variables: community wealth, police expenditure, and accessibility to major urban center. A developed area is defined as municipal land area in acres (excluding bodies of water) forests, farms, vacant land, and state parks. Valuation of developed area is the real estate valuation density of a developed area, which indicates the wealth of the community and the intensity of development (including only residential, commercial, and industrial structures which might become targets for criminals). The market value of real estate for the relevant municipalities is calculated by dividing the assessment of each community by the state computed equalization ratio. This method of calculation overcomes differences in local taxation practices. Table 2 shows that expenditures on police, property crimes, and valuation of developed areas are higher in suburban, historical core, and suburban accessible communities in Camden County, (type 1 communities) than in their counterparts (type 2 communities). Thus, wealthy, accessible suburbs suffer more crimes even though they spend more on policing than their counterparts.

Table 2 indicates that historical-core and suburban-accessible communities in Camden County spend the most on police services, have the greatest number of property offenses, and also are more affluent than any other defined subgroup of communities. Furthermore, if the relative differences between the subgroups in each classification are compared (i.e., the ratio of historical-core to non-historical core, suburban to rural etc.), the suburban-rural classification seems to be the most distant in all three variables. Comparing columns 3, 5, and 7 indicates that type 1 communities spend relatively more on policing than their wealth and their property crime level. Their share in property crime is greater than their higher wealth status.

Thus, type 1 communities spend relatively more than their counterparts on police services, are wealthier (i.e., provide more crime opportunities), and suffer more property

TABLE 2
Police Expenditures and Property Crimes Per Developed Area—Comparative Analysis

Clusters of Municipalities No. (1)	Police Expenditures Mean (in dollars) (2)	Police Expenditures Ratio[a] $(Y_{i1}/Y_{(i+1)1})$ (3)	Property Crimes Mean (4)	Property Crimes Ratio[a] $(Y_{i2}/Y_{(i+1)2})$ (5)	Valuation of Developed Area Mean (in thousands of dollars) (6)	Valuation of Developed Area Ratio[a] $(Y_{i3}/Y_{(i+1)3})$ (7)
Entire Region	107.37		0.1242		37.05	
1. Suburban (Y_{1j})	145.31	3.115	0.1636	2.678	47.02	2.23
2. Rural (Y_{2j})	46.65	1.000	0.0611	1.000	21.10	1.00
3. Historical Core[b] (Y_{3j})	197.09	2.198	0.2074	1.924	58.21	1.77
4. Non-Historical Core (Y_{4j})	89.66	1.000	0.1078	1.000	32.88	1.00
5. Suburban Accessible in Camden County[c] Communities (Y_{5j})	182.36	2.266	0.2191	2.366	55.03	1.76
6. All Other Communities (Y_{6j})	80.47	1.000	0.0926	1.000	31.20	1.00

a. The ratio is obtained as follows: $Y_{ij}/Y_{(i+1)j}$,

where $j = 1$: police expenditure per developed area; $j = 2$: number of property crimes per developed area; $j = 3$: state equalized assessed valuation excluding water bodies, forests, farms vacant land and state parks per acre developed area; i = uneven row (1, 3, 5, 7).

$(i + 1)$ = even row (2, 4, 6, 8), respectively with above uneven numbers.

b. Historical core communities are those located in Camden County along the major and historical route from Philadelphia to Atlantic City (R. 30) (15 cases) (spatial categorization).

c. This classification includes 26 of 37 Camden County municipalities. It is a cross-classification of suburban communities, adjacent to arterial routes within 14 miles from the two cities—Philadelphia and Camden (functional and spatial categorization).

crimes. The ratio of suburban to rural communities for police expenditures is greater than the property crime ratio, and the latter ratio is greater than the wealth ratio. The same phenomenon appears between the other group of communities: property crime is relatively higher in type 1 communities even though they spend relatively more on policing.

Suburban communities are relatively homogeneous in their population composition, especially with regard to socioeconomic status, which tends to be higher than in any other areas. Once it is assumed that the wealthier people are the less they are likely to commit property offenses, these findings lead us to attribute the high level of crime in the wealthy suburbs to out-of-town offenders. In short, wealthy suburbs mostly import their offenders from neighboring communities or urban areas.

Comparing type 1 communities to type 2 communities reveals that wealth in its various forms (e.g., commercial establishment, houses with expensive contents) attracts criminals. Wealthy places attract more crimes than their share in wealth, regardless of the higher share of police expenditure. This result implies that suburban police are somewhat ineffective in combatting crime. These results may not refer to offender data due to the low clearance rate in this region (14%). Reliance on specific criminal data may produce biased results because such low clearance rate may not represent the whole population of offenders.

POLICE EXPENDITURE AND CRIME: CONTROLLING FOR INTERJURISDICTIONAL WEALTH DIFFERENCES

The previous section indicated the important role wealth plays in attracting crime to suburban communities. Standardization of police expenditures by wealth (i.e., equalized assessed real estate valuation of developed areas) allows us to compare communities according to the emphasis they place on police services, independent of inflation and their ability to pay (Tables 3 and 4). Although the value of wealth

TABLE 3
Number of Property Crimes/Equalized Assessed Valuation
of Developed Area[a] (Mean Values)

Grouping of Municipalities	1967	1969	1970	1971	1972
1. All Municipalities					
Mean	2.76	3.36	3.27	3.28	4.25
Standard Deviation	1.49	1.77	1.78	1.66	2.08
2. Suburban/rural					
a) Suburban					
Mean	2.83	3.52	3.55	3.52	4.42
Standard Deviation	1.60	1.73	1.81	1.57	2.12
b) Rural					
Mean	2.64	3.09	2.80	2.87	2.96
Standard Deviation	1.29	1.82	1.65	1.74	2.00
3. Wealth[b]					
a) Affluent (A $45,000)					
Mean	2.78	3.43	3.33	3.51	4.27
Standard Deviation	1.88	1.85	1.76	1.67	2.07
b) Less Affluent (A $45,000)					
Mean	2.75	3.32	3.24	3.15	4.24
Standard Deviation	1.24	1.73	1.81	1.65	2.10

Source: New Jersey Attorney General, Uniform Crime Reports, State of New Jersey, 1967-1972. Division of Local Government Services, Statements of Financial Conditions of Counties and Municipalities, New Jersey Department of Community Affairs, Annual Reports 1967-1972.
a. All values are multiplied by 100,000.
b. A is equalized assessed real estate valuation of developed area per one acre developed area.

varies over the years, property offenses remain relatively constant but are higher in suburban and suburban-accessible areas than for other communities. An increase in police expenditure over time does not seem to influence the level of crime even though these communities spend a higher proportion of their budget on police protection than their counterparts. These findings suggest that wealth and accessibility attract external offenders more than the presence of police deters.

SIGNIFICANCE TESTING

The preceeding section dealt with variables considered most important in our model: police expenditure, wealth, and accessibility. This section presents statistical signifi-

TABLE 4
Police Expenditure/Equalized Assessed Valuation
of Developed Area[a] (Mean Values)

Grouping of Municipalities	1967	1969	1970	1971	1972
1. All Municipalities					
Mean	2.10	2.43	2.54	2.57	3.40
Standard Deviation	1.25	1.49	1.50	1.47	1.92
2. Suburban/rural					
a) Suburban					
Mean	2.56	2.91	3.00	3.02	3.82
Standard Deviation	1.06	1.25	1.32	1.30	1.81
b) Rural					
Mean	1.32	1.61	1.76	1.82	2.68
Standard Deviation	1.17	1.54	1.49	1.46	1.90
3. Wealth[b]					
a) Affluent (A $45,000)					
Mean	2.82	3.17	3.22	3.23	4.03
Standard Deviation	0.91	0.94	0.94	0.88	1.28
b) Less Affluent (A $45,000)					
Mean	1.81	2.03	2.17	2.22	3.06
Standard Deviation	1.24	1.59	1.62	1.61	2.12
4. Functional-Spatial					
a) Suburban-accessible in Camden County					
Mean	2.62	3.04	3.13	3.10	4.11
Standard Deviation	1.05	1.16	1.20	1.15	1.92
b) Other Communities					
Mean	1.76	1.96	2.05	2.14	2.67
Standard Deviation	1.24	1.50	1.53	1.58	1.68

Source: Division of Local Government Services, Statements of Financial Conditions of Counties and Municipalities, New Jersey Department of Community Affairs, Annual Reports 1967-1972.
a. All values are multiplied by 10,000.
b. A is equalized assessed real estate valuation of developed area per one acre developed area.

cance testing and incorporates other variables hypothesized to interact with those previously analyzed.

We are concerned about the possible reciprocal relation between property crime and police expenditure. Ignoring for the moment the relation between police activity and reporting crime, it is expected that the more money that is spent on policing, the lower the crime level. Also, the higher the crime rate, the more communities will spend on policing. Also, the higher the crime rate, the more communities will spend on policing. Thus, police expenditure and crime level are endogenous variables in the system and should be considered simultaneously. This approach was taken in several studies (e.g., Chapman, 1976; Carr Hill et al., 1973) which sought unbiased estimates for the coefficient of the variables interacting in the system. These studies were concerned with crime generation (sociological, psychological, ecological) which is not incorporated in our model. The crime equations between these studies and the present one will therefore probably differ somewhat.

The two cross-section simultaneous equations are: (1) $C/D = f_1 (X/D, W/D, COM/D)$; (2) $X/D = f_2 (C/D, W/D, POP/D, S/TH)$ (contact authors concerning the econometric model; Johnston, 1972, Ch. 12-13). We hypothesize the relationships for the above two equations as follows. Where in the crime function (equation 1): C = number of property offenses (breaking and entering, robbery, larceny of $50 and over, and auto theft). D = municipal land area in acres, excluding water bodies, forest farms, vacant land, and state parks. C/D = the intensiveness of property crimes in the community. X/D = police expenditure per acre developed area, which indicate the intensiveness of policing in the developed part of the municipality. Since these small suburban police departments spend most of their budget on manpower (80%) and the portion of nonpersonnel is very small in small communities, it is reasonable to assume that police expenditure is a good proxy for patrolmen. Thus, the more patrolmen there are, the less property crime is likely to occur. W/D = valuation of equalized real estate per acre of developed area. This variable expresses the wealth of the community. The wealthier a community is, the more opportunities it offers, and the more crime it is expected to attract. COM/D = percentage commercial land use of total developed area. Commercial goods are especially valuable to offenders due to their high resale value (Klockars, 1974). Also, shoplifting, larcenies from parked cars at shopping centers, and auto theft are common offenses in suburban shopping centers. Thus the more commercial land use is present, the higher is expected to be the level of property crime.

The analysis in the preceding sections suggested that accessible communities are wealthier than nonaccessible communities, a phenomenon well documented in empirical studies of the location theory (e.g., Alonso, 1965: Chs. 4, 5). The high correlation between these two variables (wealth and accessibility) should be avoided to prevent severe multi-collineary problems in the statistical regression model.

In the police expenditure function (equation 2): C/D = the more property crimes exist, the more pressure is exerted by constituents on their representatives to increase police expenditures (demand variable). W/D = the wealthier a community is, the more taxes are collected, and the more will be spent on all public services, including police (supply variable). POP = the population size. POP/D = net population density. The density level is associated with the level of police expenditures, i.e., the higher the density level, the more police expenditure is necessary to provide the same per capita level of security and safety (supply variable; see, for example, Task Force Report: Police, 1967). S = the number of dwelling units in single and two-family unit buildings. TH = total number of dwelling units including dwelling units in single and two-family unit buildings, dwelling units in multifamily structures and mobile homes. S/TH = the portion of the population which is relatively immobile due to their investment in more permanent housing arrangements (e.g., due to ownership). It is assumed that those residents who are less mobile are more concerned with the safety of their neighborhood than are those who are more mobile or whose residence in the area is temporary (Ross, 1977). People living in single two-unit dwellings have more children to protect, and therefore require more safety and protection. We prefer to use housing ratio rather than population ratio (i.e., the proportion of population residing in single two-family units of the total population) because the former better represents the voters' power and influence in these matters. Using the ratio of population may distort the nature and extent of voters' power because the number of children, who do not have voting rights, may be higher in single two-family homes than in other forms of housing. In other words, political pressure is exerted mostly by the adult population. We therefore expect that the higher the population size of single two-unit dwellings in the housing stock, the more it will spend on police (demand variable).

The importance of solving these equations in a system framework is not only to improve the parameter estimates so that it becomes possible to predict the property crime level, knowing the (dual) interrelationship of C/D and X/D, but also to provide a theoretical interpretation of the results.

RESULTS

Table 5 presents the regression results of the reduced form equation, the OLS expenditure function, and the second state of the corrected property crime equation.

The results of the two-stage least-square regression provide statistical significance for our earlier findings and, thus, strengthen them. Wealth and commercial concentration are positively related to property crime level and may be the reasons for the attraction of criminals to suburbs.

Police expenditure appears insignificantly rather than negatively related to property crime in the crime equation (equation 3, Table 5). This theoretically unexpected result has also been found in other empirical studies, and several attempts to account for it have been made (McPheters et al., 1974; Zipin et al., 1974). It seems that the police are not successful in preventing crime because they lack the necessary resources, and cannot deter offenders, particularly professional ones. We have also suggested that the high correlation between police expenditure and the crime level in suburban communities may be accounted for by the wealth of the community (the intervening variable) rather than by some direct relation between the crime level and police expenditure. That is, wealthy communities attract more crime, and as police expenditure is a constant percentage of their budget, the wealthier they are, the higher will be the amount spent on police.

TABLE 5
Regression Results

Equation Number	Description	Intercept	$\frac{C}{D}$	$\frac{\hat{X}}{D}$ [a]	$\frac{W}{D}$	$\frac{COM}{D}$	$\frac{POP}{D}$	$\frac{S}{TH}$	F	R^2	df
1	Reduced form of police expenditure function	−105.09 (−2.98)			2.50 (8.25)	7.4331* (1.80)	3.65 (4.16)	0.7487 (2.04)	78.08	0.78	89
2	Police expenditure function—regular OLS (ordinary least-square)	−107.12 (−3.07)	207.43 (3.48)		1.72 (4.08)		7.46 (3.47)	0.83 (2.28)	86.22	0.80	89
3	Second stage crime equation	0.01146* (0.66)		0.0006* (1.82)	0.000039 (2.03)	0.0305 (3.92)			56.50	0.65	90

*Coefficient is insignificant at the .05 probability level.

a. $\frac{\hat{X}}{D}$ is predicted value of $\frac{X}{D}$ obtained in the first stage of the 2SLS estimation.

This analysis points to the effect that wealth and accessibility have on the crime level. They appear to be strong incentives for offenders to operate in suburbs, which are wealthier and more accessible, rather than in rural or suburban places which are less accessible to the urban centers. Moreover, the relatively stronger and more concentrated efforts of large city police forces add impetus to offenders to shift their operation to the suburbs. These factors which express attractions to offenders (wealth and accessibility) in the statistical analysis seem to override the net effect of suburban police deterrence.

SUMMARY, CONCLUSIONS, AND POLICY IMPLICATIONS

This study has been an attempt to explain the spatial distribution of property offenses by using a geoeconomic approach. Accordingly, an offender will try to maximize his net benefits (i.e., total benefits minus total costs). The expected illegal income from the offense is the benefit, while the costs are composed of the consequences of distance or accessibility to the crime target (e.g., explicit transportation costs, set up costs of getting familiar with the target area), and the probability of apprehension, as indicated by police expenditures.

We presented evidence that urban centers are less wealthy than suburbs and spend more money on policing, a fact which may encourage the potential offender to shift his operation to the suburbs. Suburbs attract offenders because: (1) commercial activity is high and involves expensive merchandise; and (2) police effectiveness is relatively low. We have also tried to show that criminals are more attracted to the wealthier and more accessible suburbs than their counterparts. Despite the fact that suburban communities spend relatively more of their budget on police, this expenditure does not reduce the high level of property offenses. We conclude, therefore, that the wealth of communities attracts potential offenders more than the efforts of the local police deter them, particularly in relation to the intensive efforts of neighboring city police departments. We have also suggested that the wealth of the communities may be the connection between the crime rate and police expenditure.

Although this study has presented mainly indirect evidence for the relation between the residence of offenders and the crime site, or the migration patterns of offenders, the findings may be useful for planning efforts to prevent and control crime. If the spatial distribution of crime is related to those forces that may attract offenders (e.g., wealth or other crime opportunities) as well as to those that may drive them out of certain areas (such as intensiveness of policing), it may be useful and efficient to coordinate the policing of adjacent communities or to consolidate some police departments, rather than to combat crime on a local jurisdictional basis alone. Under the current situation, big city police forces spend most of their budget on patrolling, which probably causes displacement of crimes from the cities to the suburbs. Coordination of efforts to combat crime should be aimed not to divert crime to areas in which the costs are lower, but in the absolute reduction of total crimes committed in the region. To substantiate these conclusions, research should analyze individual criminal mobility. Crime attitudes and demographic data should be collected on arrested offenders to understand better their mobility and motivations for migrating from an urban residence to a suburban crime site.

REFERENCES

ALONSO, W. (1965) Location and Land Use. Cambridge, MA: Harvard Univ. Press.

BEASLEY, R. W. and G. ANTUNES (1974) "The etiology of urban crime: an ecological analysis." Criminology 11: 439-461.

BECKER, G. (1968) "Crime and punishment—an economic approach." J. of Pol. Economy 76: 169-217.

BOGGS, S. L. (1965) "Urban crime patterns." Amer. Soc. Rev. 30: 899-908.

BORDUA, D. J. (1958) "Juvenile delinquency and anomie: an attempt at replication." Social Problems 6: 230-238.

BRUTON, M. J. (1975) Introduction to Transportation Planning. London: Hutchinson & Co.

CARR HILL, R. A. and N. H. STERN (1973) "An econometric model of the supply and control of recorded offenses in England and Wales." J. of Public Economics 2(4): 289-318.

CHAIKEN, J. M. (1974) The Impact of Police Activity on Crime: Robberies in the New York City Subway System. New York: Rand Institute.

CHAPMAN, J. I. (1976) "An economic model of crime and police: some empirical results." J. of Research in Crime and Delinquency 13(1): 48-63.

DEFLEUR, L. B. (1967) "Ecological variables in the cross-cultural study of delinquency," in H. L. Voss and D. M. Peterson (eds.) Ecology, Crime and Delinquency. New York: Appleton-Century-Croft.

EHRLICH, I. (1972) "The deterrent effects of criminal law enforcement." J. of Legal Studies 1(2): 259-276.

HUNT, L. A. and K. WEINER (1977) "The impact of juvenile curfew suppression and displacement in patterns of juvenile offenses." J. of Police Sci. and Administration 5(4): 707-712.

McPHETERS, L. R. and W. B. STRONGE (1974) "Law enforcement expenditures and urban crime." National Tax J. 27(4): 633-644.

MEHAY, S. L. (1977) "Interjurisdictional spillover of urban police service." Southern Econ. J. 43(3): 1352-1359.

PALMER, J. (1977) "Economic analyses of the deterrent effect of punishment: a review." J. of Research in Crime and Delinquency 14(1): 4-21.

President's Commission on Law Enforcement and Administration of Justice (1967) Task Force Report: The Police. Washington, DC: Government Printing Office.

PYLE, G. F. (1974) The Spatial Dynamic of Crime. Chicago: University of Chicago, Department of Geography Research Paper no. 159: 129-141.

QUINNEY, R. (1964) "Crime, delinquency and social areas." J. of Research in Crime and Delinquency 1: 149-154.

RAND CORPORATION (1971) Some Effects of an Increase in Police Manpower in the 20th Precinct of New York City. New York: Rand Corporation.

RENGERT, G. F. (1977) "Burglary in Philadelphia: a critique on an opportunity structure model." Presented at the Annual Meeting of the Association of American Geographers, Salt Lake City, Utah.

REPPETTO, T. A. (1976) "Crime prevention and the displacement phenomenon." Crime and Delinquency 22(2): 166-177.

ROSS, M. (1950) Economic Opportunity and Crime. Montreal: Renouf Publishing Co.

ROBINSON, W. S. (1950) "Ecological correlations and the behavior of individuals." Amer. Soc. Rev. 15: 351-357.

SHAW, C. R. and H. D. MCKAY (1942) Juvenile Delinquency and Urban Areas. Chicago: Univ. of Chicago Press.

SCHMID, C. F. (1960) "Urban crime areas: Part I." Amer. Soc. Rev. 25: 527-542.

SCHMID, C. F. (1960) "Urban crime areas: Part II." Amer. Soc. Rev. 25: 655-678.

ZIPIN, P. M., R. H. MABRY, and C. L. DYER (1974) "Crime rates and public expenditures for police protection: a comment." Rev. of Social Economy, 32(2): 222-225.

Carl E. Pope
University of Wisconsin—Milwaukee

3

VICTIMIZATION RATES AND NEIGHBORHOOD CHARACTERISTICS
Some Preliminary Findings

Since the advent of the first victimization surveys in the mid-sixties, interest has centered on the development of such surveys and the use of information derived from them. As a supplement to official statistics, victim surveys provide critical information about victimization experiences and the risk of victimization that is not available elsewhere. Research findings derived from these surveys have ranged from public attitudes toward the police to the potential of restitution programs for both personal and household crimes. Interest has also centered on a comparison of victim survey results and official crime statistics, especially those generated by the Uniform Crime Reporting System. A third area— and perhaps the most topical—has been the reevaluation and refinement of different methodological aspects of victim surveys. With regard to overall victimization rates, attention has primarily concerned the individual characteristics of those victimized by crime. These rates vary by such individual characteristics as age, race, and income. Similarly, the demographic characteristics of those offenders engaged

AUTHOR'S NOTE: *This article was originally prepared for presentation at the 1978 meetings of the American Society of Criminology, Dallas, Texas. This analysis was made possible through a grant to the Criminal Justice Research Center, Albany, New York, from the Statistics Division of the National Criminal Justice Information and Statistics Service, Law Enforcement Assistance Administration, United States Department of Justice.*

in personal crime against victim respondents have also been explored. An examination of victimization rates by neighborhood or areal characteristics, however, has been generally ignored by victimization researchers.

Historically, ecological or social area studies of crime and delinquency have yielded much needed and useful information. The ecological approach adopted by the Chicago School in the early 1930s produced a large body of research findings and furnished the empirical foundation for some major criminological theories (Shaw and McKay, 1972; Faris and Dunham, 1965; Short, 1976). For example, rates of crime and delinquency were found to decrease as the distance from the center of the city increased with the "zone in transition" consistently yielding the highest rate. Further, these rates tended to remain high despite changes in the composition of the population. With regard to specific offenses, higher rates for personal violent crime such as homicide and aggravated assault were prevalent in residential areas of the city characterized as socially disorganized. These areas had distinct ethnic compositions and low socioeconomic status. However, evidence does suggest that ethnicity and socioeconomic status are not related to the distribution of crime in an identical manner. Most ecological findings, such as those noted above, are based on official data sources in the form of arrest statistics. Alternative indices have not adequately been examined as a source of knowledge regarding crime distributions and areal characteristics.

This essay attempts to explore the relation between victimization rates and selected neighborhood characteristics by examining National Crime Survey data from 1973 to 1976. Simply put, we address ourselves to the question of how much of the variation in household victimization rates (consisting of burglary, larceny, and auto theft) can be attributed to the respondent's neighborhoods. The results of such undertakings may have practical as well as theoretical significance. If, for example, household victimization rates vary by neighborhood characteristics, then implications may be drawn regarding crime prevention strategies. Further, if patterns are similar to those concerning official data and ecological characteristics, then theoretical perspectives found on such relationships will be given added support.

PREVIOUS VICTIMIZATION FINDINGS

Throughout the 1970s a rather large volume of research literature accumulated that concerned criminal victimization in major American cities and on a national probability basis as well. While the bulk of this research examined victim characteristics of household heads, the results are quite informative. In a summary report analyzing victim survey results in eight impact cities, Hindelang (1974) found that the total household victimization rate was 465 per 1000 households (about one victimization for every two households) for the twelve month period covered by the survey. With regard to race and family income, the data showed that blacks/others in every income category (except $25,000 or more) had total household victimization rates at least slightly greater than households headed by whites (Hindeland, 1974: 30). Further white household heads evidenced higher victimization rates for larceny, while blacks/others incurred higher rates for burglary and auto theft—a relationship that held across income categories. These data also revealed that total household victimization rates had a strong inverse relation to the age of household heads (Hindelang, 1974: 34).

Selected results highlighted in a national survey of criminal victimization for burglary, larceny, and motor vehicle theft revealed the following:

> For two forms of household burglary, blacks had a higher rate than whites; as a result, the overall rate for that crime was much higher among blacks.
> For each of the three forms of household crime, rates of victimization generally declined as the age of the head of the household increased.

The poorest householders had the lowest rates for motor vehicle thefts; however, there was no apparent relationship between income and the incidence of household larceny or burglary.
The rates for household larceny and motor vehicle theft tended to increase as the number of persons per household increased. For each of the three household crimes, white renters had a substantially higher rate than white homeowners; among blacks, however, this pattern failed to apply. Black homeowners recorded higher rates for burglary and motor theft than did white homeowners.
Black renters had a higher burglary rate than white renters, but the opposite was true with respect to household larceny [National Crime Survey Report, 1975: 6].

In sum, blacks, younger individuals, renters, and members of large households were differentially affected by household property crimes.

In a recent monograph, Gibbs (1976) examined household victimization rates, individual characteristics of victims, and degree of urbanization. Based on an analysis of the 1974 National Crime Survey data, this study showed that as the extent of urbanization increased so did the probability of victimization. Moreover, larger victimization differences were noted between suburban and rual areas than between urban and suburban areas. With regard to race, both urban and rural areas exhibited similar victimization rates, while in suburban areas the black/other rate was one-third larger (Gibbs, 1976: 10). While age and income differences were also noted in household victimization rates, "rate differences among the population areas [were] for the most, independent of the characteristics of victims" (Gibbs, 1976: 36).

In a similar study, Shichor, Decker, and O'Brien (n.d.) used 1974 victim survey data compiled from twenty-six large American cities to examine the relation between population density and criminal victimization. Rather than observing an overall positive relationship between crime and population density (as much of the previous research

literature suggested), the authors found that the relationship depended on the type of offense involved. More
specifically, in examining ten separate offenses, a positive
relationship held only for property crimes with contact. In
all other instances, the association between victimization
offense and population density was negative (Shichor,
et al., n.d.)

NATIONAL CRIME SURVEY DATA

As noted above, this analysis employs National Crime
Survey data collected on a national basis from 1973
through 1976. These victimization data were compiled by
the Bureau of Census in cooperation with the Law Enforcement Assistance Administration, and include probability
estimates for the entire population. Approximately 60,000
households were surveyed each year and the respondents
were asked to provide rather detailed information about
victimization experiences within the past six months, and a
variety of household characteristics such as family income,
age of the household head, and the like. Also appended to
the national sample is information pertaining to the area in
which the respondent resides.

The dependent variables for the analysis reported herein consist of household victimization rates for burglary,
larceny, and auto theft—property offenses which generally
involve no contact between victim and perpetrator. The independent variables include selected neighborhood characteristics. Over forty neighborhood characteristics were provided
in the national samples including the following illustrative
types:

(1) Income level—families with less than $5,000 family income
as a proportion of total families.
(2) Mobility—persons five years of age and older living in the
same household as of five years ago as a proportion of total
persons five years of age and older.
(3) Population Characteristics—population aged 0-7 as a proportion of the total population.

(4) Educational Level—median years of school completed for persons aged 25-54 years.

(5) Employment—unemployed persons 16 years of age or more as a proportion of the total civilian labor force 16 years of age or more.

(6) Race—black population as a proportion of the total population.

(7) Housing—owner occupied housing units as a proportion of total occupied housing units.

Since it would be virtually impossible to examine the relation between household victimization rates and all neighborhood characteristics, those dealing with specific population characteristics were chosen for analysis. This was done for two reasons. First, previous research demonstrated a positive relation between victimization rates and degree of urbanization (Gibbs, 1976) and a negative relation between victimization rates (except for property crimes with contact) and population density (Shichor, et al., n.d.). Since those data contain ecological information dealing with population factors, it might be possible to shed additional light on these previous findings. Second, the population data allow us to examine two extreme distributions where variations would be more likely to occur. These include the percentage of the population aged 0-17 and aged 65 and over as a proportion of the total population. Also included is the percentage of families with a female head as a proportion of all families.

The independent variables were trichotomized into distinct categories of low, medium, and high. A fourth category includes those instances where relevant information was not ascertained. The three categories for the first variable are: (1) areas where 0-29% of the population is aged 0-17; (2) areas where 20-39% of the population is aged 0-17; and areas in which 40 or more percent of the population is aged 0-17. The second variable—aged 65 and over—contains the following areal distribution: 0-5%; 6-12%; and 13+%. Corresponding cutting points for those families with a female head are: 0-5%; 6-12%; and 17+%.

ANALYSIS

Tables 1, 2, and 3 present bivariate relationships between victimization rates for burglary, larceny, and motor vehicle theft, and the three neighborhood characteristics selected for analysis. Examination of Table 1 reveals that as the percentage of the population age 0-17 increases, so does the larceny victimization rate from a low of 104.2 per 1000 households to a high of 142.5 per 1000 households. For both larceny and burglary the highest victimization rates occur in areas where over 40% of the population is aged 17 years or under. For auto theft the opposite is true. Here victimization rates are slightly higher in areas with the lowest percentage of the population under age 17. Interestingly, both burglary and motor vehicle theft victimization rates are lowest in the mid category where between 30 and 39% of the population is aged 17 years or less.

Table 2 repeats the analysis for areas with varying proportions of elderly residents. All three victimization rates tend to decline as the percentage of the population aged 65 or older increases. The decline is most substantial for larceny followed by burglary and motor vehicle theft. This finding lends some support to the observation that while the elderly are more fearful of being victimized, they are less likely to actually suffer a victimization. It must be kept in mind, however, that these data are based on areal, not individual, characteristics.

Table 3 reveals some interesting patterns. As the percentage of neighborhoods with female heads of families increases so does the household victimization rate. This trend is opposite to that noted previously for areas with a high percentage of elderly residents. The most notable increase occurs for burglary victimization rates. In those areas with less than 5% of families with female heads, the burglary victimization rate is 81.1 per 1000 households compared to a rate of 130.9 for those areas where 17% or more of the households are headed by a female. This greater vulnerability to burglary victimization may be related to a high proportion of working mothers, in which case

TABLE 1
Household Victimization Rates by the Percentage of the
Population Aged 0-17 as a Proportion of the Total Population
(rates per 1,000 households)

Type of Crime	0–29 (3,618,056)	30–39 (7,559,830)	40–99 (3,757,287)	NA (1,880,873)
Burglary	94.7 (1,555,591)	84.8 (3,012,489)	101.6 (1,453,784)	100.3 (652,994)
Larcency	104.2 (1,710,777)	111.4 (3,957,612)	142.5 (2,038,343)	167.0 (1,086,865)
Motor Vehicle Theft	21.4 (351,689)	16.6 (589,728)	18.5 (265,160)	21.7 (141,014)

Note: Numbers in parentheses refer to households in the group.

TABLE 2
Household Victimization Rates by the Percentage of the
Population Aged 65 and over as a Proportion of the Total Population
(rate per 1,000 households)

Type of Crime	0–5 (3,572,662)	6–12 (7,343,416)	13–99 (4,019,095)	NA (1,880,873)
Burglary	109.7 (1,333,051)	87.9 (2,975,013)	84.6 (1,713,800)	100.3 (652,994)
Larceny	162.3 (1,972,990)	111.3 (3,766,669)	97.1 (1,967,073)	167.0 (1,086,865)
Motor Vehicle Theft	21.9 (266,621)	17.8 (601,734)	16.7 (338,221)	21.7 (141,014)

Note: Numbers in parentheses refer to households in the group.

there would be a large number of unattended residences.
Again, the data are only suggestive and do not allow us to
directly examine this hypothesis.

SUMMARY AND DISCUSSION

At this point our preliminary analysis suggests that
household victimization rates vary by the specific population

TABLE 3
Household Victimization Rates by the Percentage of Families
with a Female Head as a Proportion of all Families
(rate per 1,000 households)

Type of Crime	0–5 (2,091,794)	6–16 (10,115,660)	17–99 (2,727,720)	NA (1,880,873)
Burglary	81.1 (810,835)	84.4 (3,920,815)	130.9 (1,290,214)	100.3 (652,994)
Larceny	112.7 (1,126,127)	116.1 (5,392,611)	120.1 (1,187,994)	167.1 (1,086,865)
Motor Vehicle Theft	15.5 (154,832)	17.3 (802,234)	25.3 (249,511)	21.7 (141,014)

Note: Numbers in parentheses refer to households in the group.

characteristics of respondent's neighborhood. Tabular results show that burglary, larceny, and motor vehicle theft victimization rates change rather markedly when we consider the proportion of the population age 17 or less, age 65 or more, and the percentage of families with a female head. For all categories, larceny victimization rates tend to be the highest, followed by burglary and motor vehicle theft rates. Larceny victimization rates tend to increase as neighborhoods contain a higher percentage of young persons and female heads of households. These rates tend to decrease, however, as neighborhoods hold a higher proportion of elderly residents.

These results are consistent with those of Gibbs (1976) who found a substantial relation between household victimization rates and the degree of urbanization. However, in that analysis this relation also held even when individual characteristics (such as race, income, and age) were introduced as control variables. A further step in this type of analysis then, would be to explore multivariate relationships among household victimization rates, neighborhood characteristics, and individual characteristics. It is quite possible that the first results comparing victimization rates and neighborhood factors may change when race, income, and age of household heads are introduced as control variables. It would also be important to explore such relationships with the remaining neighborhood characteristics since the analysis reported herein was limited to three specific population characteristics. While the findings reported here are indeed promising, much more work needs to be undertaken in examining neighborhood characteristics and criminal victimization rates. Data currently collected by the Bureau of Census under the National Crime Survey should provide a strong foundation.

REFERENCES

FARIS, R.E.L., and W. DUNHAM (1965) Mental Disorders in Urban Areas (rev. ed.). Chicago: Univ. of Chicago Press.

GIBBS, J. J. (1976) Household Victimization Rates and Characteristics of Victims In Urban, Suburban and Rural Areas: A Comparative Analysis. Analytic Report #8, Criminal Justice Research Center, Albany, New York.

HINDELANG, M. J. (1976) Criminal Victimization in Eight American Cities. Cambridge, MA: Ballinger.

——— (1974) An Analysis of Victimization Survey Results from the Eight Impact Cities: Summary Report. U.S. Department of Justice: Government Printing Office.

——— and J. GAROFALO (1977) An Introduction to the National Crime Survey. Analytic Report #7, Criminal Justice Research Center, Albany, New York.

SHAW, C. R., and H. D. McKAY (1972) Juvenile Delinquency and Urban Areas (rev. ed.). Chicago: Univ. of Chicago Press.

SHICHOR, D., D. T. DECKER, and R. M. O'BRIEN (n.d.) An Empirical Analysis of Population Density and Criminal Victimization in Central Cities: Some Unexpected Findings. California State College, San Bernadino. (unpublished)

SHORT, J. F. [ed.] (1976) Delinquency, Crime and Society. Chicago: Univ. of Chicago Press.

U.S. Department of Justice (1976) A National Crime Survey Report on Criminal Victimization in the United States 1975, U.S. Department of Justice: Government Printing Office.

William E. Berg
University of Wisconsin—Milwaukee

Robert Johnson
American University

4

ASSESSING THE IMPACT OF VICTIMIZATION
Acquisition of the Victim Role Among Elderly and Female Victims

It is generally assumed that crime represents a special problem for those groups that are the most vulnerable to certain types or patterns of victimization. This has been the case, for example, among the elderly where vulnerability has been associated with a range of physical, social, and economic factors which define the position of the elderly in our society; and it has generally been the case among female victims, where many of these same factors come into play along with sexual vulnerability (Amir, 1971; Goldsmith and Goldsmith, 1975). Much of the literature on patterns of victimization among the elderly and women suggests, moreover, that even though the absolute incidence of crime against them may be lower than the incidence for young males (U.S. Department of Justice, 1975: 21), the fact that they are victimized acquires greater significance for them than it does for other groups. From this perspective the problem is not one of distinguishing patterns of victimization, but of identifying the effect of this experience.

In examining this effect, considerable emphasis has been placed on what is perhaps the most immediate and transparent outcome of the experience, that is, on the "fear of crime" syndrome. A number of studies have shown signifi-

cant correlations between the victimization experience and
subsequent feelings of fear or peril (Antunes et al., 1977).
Among the elderly, the evidence suggests that this fear is
not restricted to actual victims, but that it has become
generalized throughout the aged population (Kahana et al.,
1977). A similar, though less pronounced, pattern of generalized fear occurs among females, both with respect to
sexual and nonsexual offenses (Smith, 1976).

The incidence of fear of crime among victims (and persons who diagnose themselves as prospective victims) is
important, not only because it is a personal reaction to what
is, after all, a frightening situation, but because it presumably leads to patterns of behavior that are designed to deal
with the problem. In some instances, these reactions prove
inadequate or even counterproductive (Antunes et al.,
1977: 326). Thus, the elderly, for example, may choose to
stay at home and withdraw from the life of the community
under the assumption that they are safer and less exposed
in their homes. While they may, in fact, be relatively safe in
their homes (at least on a statistical basis), they pay a
substantial price for this security in terms of lost or spoiled
social contacts and supports. Perhaps more importantly,
when crime follows them into their homes (Antunes et al.,
1977: 327), the self-defined prisoners are often left with no
havens of safety at all.

The present study is an attempt to deal, both conceptually
and empirically, with some of the issues involved in the
analysis of the victim role. Victimological research has
principally explored the "role and responsibility of the
victim" in precipitating the offense (Schafer, 1976: 143).
The work of Lamborn (1968) for example, uses a "victim
orientation"—which includes distinct levels of responsibilities—to examine the role the victim plays in providing
justification for the offense. Much of this work derives,
directly or indirectly, from the earlier work of Von Hentig
(1948) on the differential susceptibility of the victim as a
function of social, psychological, and physical characteristics. The study used Mendelsohn's (1963) typology of
the victim-offender relationship in terms of levels of legal

responsibility or involvement, and Wolfgang's (1958) analysis of "victim-precipitated" homicides. These approaches suggest what may, however, be a limited view of the victim role. They emphasize those attributes of the victim that relate to level of involvement in criminal victimization (Hindelang, 1976: 18) and functional responsibility for the offense (Schafer, 1968), while they de-emphasize or ignore distinctions that arise in the subsequent behavior and adjustment of the victim. Yet it stands to reason that, as victims vary in the social, psychological, and physical resources they bring to the offense, they will also vary in their response to the offense; that is, they will vary in the extent and manner in which they adopt a victim role as a consequence of criminal victimization. To the extent that this process operates, it indicates the costs of victimization that occur above and beyond tangible or immediate loss or discomfort, and highlights the effects of victimization that may need to be considered in programs designed to assist or compensate the victims of crime.

THE VICTIM ROLE AND ITS ACQUISITIONS

The victim role is similar to the other social roles. For our purposes, we may define a role as a set of expectations impinging on an incumbent of a social position (Biddle and Thomas, 1966). These expectations are about how a person should behave in a particular position, about the attitudes and values considered appropriate to the position, and about the specific knowledge, skills, or attributes required of the individual in a particular position. In this sense, for example, persons who are medical doctors in our society are confronted with relatively clear directives regarding appropriate professional and personal deportment. Victims of crime may be similarly influenced by expectations regarding their behavior, though these prescriptions have never been clearly distinguished. At a minimum, victims are expected to act like persons who have been violated or compromised. Shock, confusion, impotent anger, or rage— even remorse and shame—are presumably appropriate sentiments. Victimization represents a concrete index of the vulnerability (to external insults) and dependence (on public officials who must ameliorate their problems or at least certify their status as victims). The prototypic victim is thus the person who acknowledges in the act and in his or her reactions to it, the inevitability and appropriateness of victimization and takes the experience to be a product of fate, however unpleasant or unjust.

The victim role, like most roles, is presumably acquired through developmental learning (cf., Olesen and Whittaker, 1968). A developmental approach to role acquisition suggests that individuals go through a process in distinct stages, and that, in each of these stages, adjustments or modifications of the role are made in accordance with individual needs and resources. Thornton and Nardi (1975) have proposed a four-stage process of role acquisition, which includes anticipation of the role, the formal acquisition of the role, the informal adjustment to the frequently subtle distinctions found in the role, and the personal adaptation of the role to inner needs and drives. Variations may occur in relation to such things as the relevance of a given role to the other roles that the individual characteristically performs within the society or the social group, or the particular skills and knowledge required by the role. Thus the individual is not as likely to reach the final stage in those instances where the role in question is markedly different from his or her role-set, and may never move beyond the anticipatory stage if the specialized skills, knowledge, or attributes necessary to the final stages of role acquisition are lacking.

The victim role is the outcome of a process that involves, at least during its initial stages, the interaction between the perceptions of the offender and certain behaviors or characteristics of the ultimate victim. The offender selects his or her victim on the basis of certain clues provided by the potential victim. Presumably these clues include the various "dispositional factors" involved in precipitating the offense (see Hindelang, 1976: 17), along with certain physical or social characteristics of the potential victim (e.g., race, age, sex, manner of appearance, or patterns of behavior). In some cases these clues may also involve the assumption that the victim is already a victim; he or she is perceived by the offender to be performing the role of victim and is, therefore, an appropriate target.

Once the victim has, in fact, become a victim, we may assume that the formal stage of role acquisition has been reached. The boundaries of the preceding stage, that of the anticipation of the role, are considerably less distinct and presumably vary widely from group to group. The anticipation of victimization is largely a function of the mass media acting in conjunction with other, less structured, sources of information. The victim role that is presented through these means is likely to be dysfunctional, in that it emphasizes a view of the world which features an "abnormally high proportion of sexy women, violent acts, and extra-legal solutions to legal problems" (Schramm, 1961: 155). The mass media is not, however, the only source of information regarding the victim role. In certain crimes, such as rape, it has been presumed that the dimensions of the victim role are susceptible to change or to manipulation by training and preparing the potential victim, or by developing community resources designed to serve the victim after the offense has been committed (see Weis and Borges, 1973). It is also clear, finally, that specific social groups develop information networks that include, particularly with the elderly, a set of presumptions about victimization (Kahana et al., 1977).

During the formal stage of role acquisition, the victim has several options. Depending on the nature of the reference group involved, the victim may or may not choose to report the crime. If the crime is reported, the role of victim tends to acquire a whole set of prescriptions which are implicit and explicit in the role-set; that is, the victim is forced to behave in a manner dictated by the behaviors of other individuals occupying positions in the criminal justice system, in the medical system (in those instances where injuries have occurred through the offense), and in many instances in an insurance system (where property has been stolen or damaged). There is a high degree of consensus within and between these systems regarding expected victim role behaviors. Conformity to these expectations may vary, as we have indicated, in relation to the cultural values of the social group and, in the general case, as a result of the victim's previous experience with the role.

Even when the victim chooses to become involved and report the offense, in this institutional network of reinforcing behaviors and expectations, wide variations may still exist in relation to the actual enactment of this role. As Parsons (1951) has observed, roles allow for variability in performance according to the different personalities and experiences of the actor. This freedom exists, in part, because the informal prescriptions attached to the victim role, or to any role, are defined in terms of "mays" rather than "musts." While the formal dimensions of the role tend to be defined in rather rigid terms (e.g., one must complete certain forms in order to meet the requirements of the insurance company), the dimensions of the informal stage provide the victim with the opportunity to shape the role and work out an individual style of role performance. In this sense, therefore, the victim may choose to invest in protecting goods or property, to alter style of life, to move to a new neighborhood, or simply to ignore the offense.

The final stage is attained when the individual has internalized the role—when he or she has psychologically adjusted or adapted to its demands (Thornton and Nardi, 1975: 880). What occurs in this stage is a process that Goffman has identified with the term "embracement": "To embrace a role is to disappear into the virtual self available in the situation, to be fully seen in terms of the image, and to conform expressively one's acceptance of it. To embrace a role is to be embraced by it" (1961: 106). In this respect the role of victim becomes personalized or embraced when the individuals reconcile their concept of themselves and the requirements of the role, a reconciliation which minimizes the distance between the two.

DIFFERENTIAL ACQUISITION OF
THE VICTIM ROLE

The victim role, like any role, allows for variations in performance and level or extent to which the role is internalized. Victims thus may vary in the degree that they embrace this role as a central feature of their lives, and they can play out the role in distinctively personal ways. While some victims may ultimately adopt the role and make it, figuratively speaking, a part of themselves, others may be uninvolved with the role and may adapt to victimization as though nothing of consequence has occurred.

The source of differences in resilience in the face of victimization may be found in the circumstances of the victims' lives and in the nature of their relations with the society. The victimization literature suggests, for example, that the elderly are more likely to feel the effects of victimization because of their relative powerlessness within the society (Goldsmith and Goldsmith, 1975: 6). The elderly tend to lose the sense of "active mastery" that generally characterizes the middle-aged persons' interaction with the society. As their ability to function effectively in the physical, social, or economic realms gradually decreases, they experience a corresponding decrease in their ability to control the contingencies affecting their lives, and they become, broadly speaking, the victims of their circumstances (Rotter, 1966). Such feelings of generic vulnerability are associated with perceptions of pervasive external threats and lead to differential reactions to victimization in terms of patterns of adjustment and adaptation. Similar observations have been made, moreover, regarding the relative power or status of women within the society, and the corollary feelings of vulnerability such positions entail (Bardwick, 1971; Gersof, 1971).

More generally, some support for the presumed link between social status or power and role acquisition is found in the literature on role-taking and the distribution of roles within social groups (Turner, 1962; Bales and Slater, 1955). Experimental research demonstrates that the assignment of new roles within a family setting is inversely related to the distribution of power within such groups: those individuals with the least power were more readily allocated new roles than those with greater power (Thomas et al., 1972). The distribution of roles within small groups is also related to the status that the individual occupies in the society (Berger et al., 1962). Thus, persons who occupy lower status positions in the external world, as measured by considerations of age, sex, and race, are more likely to perform lower status roles within the group than those who occupy higher status positions in the external world.

What all of this suggests is a framework to develop a model of the differential acquisition of the victim role. The model is derived from role theory, and specifically from a developmental approach to role acquisition. The model assumes that the emergence of the victim role is one effect of victimization, an effect that may not be as transparent or immediate as those associated with property loss or physical injury, but one which may be useful to analyze the long-run adjustment and adaptation of the victim.

The components of this model may be explored through a hypothesis which suggests that individuals or groups who occupy lower status positions within the society (positions that are characterized by a sense of powerlessness and by the lack of available alternative roles), will be more likely to embrace the victim role than those individuals or groups who occupy higher status positions. Such persons are more likely to feel the effect of victimization because it conforms to their expectations of the society. That is, persons who occupy low status positions are more likely to see themselves as powerless and to assume that the effective control over their lives resides, not in their abilities or strengths, but in a range of external factors and forces which operate independent of their own wishes or desires (Rotter, 1966).

At this level, the model suggests that the victim role is, for these groups at least, the logical extension of their position in the society. Since they are victims of the society, in the broadest sense of the term, there is very little dissonance associated with the victim role (Ryan, 1971). In Hallie's terms, it is more likely that these groups will be subject to routine "institutionalized victimization," and thus the fact that they are involved in "personal victimization" is not inconsistent with their role in the society (1971: 257). In this respect, at least, it is possible to embrace the victim role because it is consistent with the expectation of the social order.

ASSESSING THE MODEL

To test some of the assumptions and implications of this model, we have attempted to construct a secondary analysis of an existing study which deals with the victims of juvenile offenders (Berg, 1976). Although the data are limited in scope and susceptibility to analysis through more sophisticated techniques, they provide a convenient opportunity to operationalize the model and to explore some of its ramifications.

The original study on which this analysis is based involved a total of 268 victims of juvenile offenders who had been apprehended and referred to juvenile court. The study deals, therefore, with known instances of victimization rather than with the total population of victims. The sample of victims included in the study was further limited by the fact that it excluded all sex offenses, and that all the offenses occurred within two months. Among those victims who were included, however, the response rate was quite high (approximately 72%) which suggests that it may be adequate for the purposes of this analysis.

In operationalizing the variables included in the model, we have assumed that lower status implies higher levels of powerlessness and that the latter can, additionally, be defined by distinctions based on age, race, and sex. If the model holds, one would expect to find that older people, racial minorities, and women are more likely to embrace the role of victim.

Three scales contained in the initial study were used in this analysis to measure changes in victim behavior and values that relate to acquisition of the victim role. The first of these provides a measure of adjustments made in the victim's life as a result of the victimization experience. This scale includes a range of explicit adjustments made by the victim to minimize the likelihood of any future offenses (e.g., purchased and carried self-protective devices, obtained insurance, improved security of the home, and so forth). This scale also includes adjustments made in the victim's characteristic pattern of interaction in the neighborhood and community (e.g., stay home at certain hours, more careful around juveniles, and more cautious in general). The second of these scales measures the level of anxiety or fear resulting from the offense. Fear or anxiety is viewed in terms of the victim's sense of security or safety in the home, the neighborhood and the community, and in relation to the degree which the victim is concerned about the safety of his or her property. The final scale used in this analysis measures the relation between the victim's estimated losses incurred as a result of the offense, and the level of compensation or restitution the victim deemed appropriate. By dividing the monetary values associated with the estimated losses into the desired financial entitlements we obtain a scale with values ranging from .01 to 1.00; the higher levels of this scale reflect substantial agreement between the estimates and the entitlements, while the lower figures presumably include the victim's adjustment of the entitlement to account for expenses that were not directly incurred in the offense itself. These expenses may be viewed as an indication of the psychological costs of the offense; they reflect elements of the total effect of the victimization experience that are not articulated through the remaining scales and are not accounted for in assessments of the tangible costs of victimization.

RESULTS

The results of this analysis suggest partial confirmation for the model. Table 1 includes a brief descriptive summary of the relations between the independent and dependent variable postulated by the model. It suggests that both the aged and women tend to experience greater life-style changes, have higher levels of anxiety, and have less agreement between the actual expenses incurred through the offense and their projected requests for compensation or restitution. It is presumed that the difference between actual and projected expenses reflects an element of the psychological costs of the victimization experience.

The findings relating to the black victims do not conform with the expectations of the model. Indeed, the data suggest that black victims are less likely to change their lives, that they are less likely to feel anxious about the victimization experience, and that their estimates of just or fair compensation conform rather closely with the actual costs they incurred as a result of the offense. These discrepancies may reflect some of the methodological problems involved in using race as an indicator of relative status or powerlessness. They may more plausibly indicate the extent to which the assumption of victimization and of powerlessness have come to dominate the world view of many lower class urban blacks and have spawned subcultural mechanisms (like the ubiquitous "cool role" and a deep and abiding respect for fate) designed to facilitate survival within a hostile, unpredictable environment. Socialization within such subcultures may produce a normalization of the victimization experience, or may at least make possible the assimilation of this experience within a pre-existing framework of resources and routines required for survival in the ghetto (Johnson, 1976).

The relations among these variables may also be expressed through regression coefficients. While we cannot make any assumption regarding the normality of the data, or in reference to their homoscedacity, it is assumed that these factors will not substantially influence the regression model (Karlinger and Pedhazur, 1973). Our approach to the regression format remains tentative, however, because we are unable to ascertain the level of measurement error or of errors in the specification of the relationships among the variables (Bornstedt and Carter, 1971). Nevertheless, the results

TABLE 1
Relationships Between Victim Status and
Patterns of Adjustment to the Victim Role

| Status | Elements of the Victim Role | | |
	(1) Life Style Changes (%)	(2) Level of Anxiety (%)	(3) Psychological Costs
Sex:			
Male	59.5	62.0	.79
Female	71.8	67.3	.21
Race:			
Black	56.5	37.0	.57
White	66.5	70.1	.45
Age:			
18-29	68.9	52.5	.47
30-39	57.8	67.2	.59
40-49	59.5	65.6	.32
50-59	62.4	66.6	.28
60 +	85.7	75.0	.21

suggest a relationship that is, except in the variable of race, consistent with the expectations of the model.

SUMMARY AND CONCLUSIONS

The effect of victimization has generally been viewed as the tangible costs involved in the offense itself, or in relation to certain psychological costs which extend beyond the terms of the experience to influence the victim's adjustment to the neighborhood, community, and society. It is generally assumed, moreover, that these costs are not constant and that they vary in distinctions of age, sex, race, or type of offense.

We have attempted to extend this approach to the study of victimization through the development of a model of the victim role. What this model suggests, in brief, is that the effect of victimization can be understood as a role acquisition process where certain individuals or groups are more likely to embrace the victim role than others and are more likely, therefore, to make those adjustments or adaptations inherent in the performance of this role. It further assumes that those groups that are most likely to adopt this role are those groups that are relatively powerless and that have, therefore, low status within the society.

Some of the dimensions of this model have been examined through the use of existing survey data detailing reactions to victimization among three relatively low status social groups: the elderly, females and blacks. The results of this analysis are mixed, but in general confirm the implications of the model. Thus, the elderly and women demonstrate behavior and values associated with the victim role, while the role-related behavior of blacks is substantially less. The unpredicted resilience to victimization shown by blacks may suggest that among populations exposed to victimization over long periods, the effect of any single offense is negligible and can be handled without the need to significantly adjust or alter one's characteristic life-style.

While the results are not conclusive, they do suggest that the model may be useful as a basis for understanding variations in the impact of victimization. Further work needs to be done before we can assume that the model reflects, theoretically or empirically, the implications of the victimization experience.

REFERENCES

AMIR, M. (1971) Patterns of Forcible Rape. Chicago: Univ. of Chicago Press.

ANTUNES, G. E., F. L. COOK, T. D. COOK, and W. G. SKOGAN (1977) "Patterns of crime against the elderly: findings from a national survey." Gerontologist 17: 321-328.

BALES, R. F. and P. SLATER (1955) "Role differentiation in small decision making groups," in T. Parsons and R. F. Bales (eds.) Family, Socialization and Interaction Process. New York: Free Press.

BARDWICK, J. (1971) The Psychology of Women. New York: Harper & Row.

BECKER, H., B. GEER, E. HUGHES, and A. STRAUSS (1961) Boys in White: Student Culture in Medical School. Chicago: Univ. of Chicago Press.;

BERG, W. E. (1976) The Costs of Victimization: A Study of Juvenile Crime and its Victims. Madison: Wisconsin Council on Criminal Justice.

BERGER, J., B. COHEN, and M. ZELDITCH, Jr. (1962) "Status characteristics and social interaction." Amer. Soc. Rev. 37: 241-255.

BIDDLE, B. and E. THOMAS (1966) Role Theory: Concepts and Research. New York: John Wiley.

BORNSTEDT, G. W. and T. M. CARTER (1971) "Robustness in regression analysis," pp. 118-146 in H. L. Costner (ed.) Sociological Methodology. San Francisco: Jossey-Bass.

GERSOF, M. (1971) Roles Women Play. Belmont, CA: Brooks Cole.

GOFFMAN, E. (1961) Encounters. Indianapolis: Bobbs-Merrill.

GOLDSMITH, J. and S. S. GOLDSMITH (1975) "Crime and the elderly: an overview," pp. 1-6 in J. Goldsmith and S. S. Goldsmith (eds.) Crime and the Elderly. Lexington, MA: D. C. Heath.

HALLIE, P. P. (1971) "Justification and rebellion," pp. 257-272 in N. Sanford and C. Comstock (eds.) Sanctions For Evil. Boston: Beacon Press.

HINDELANG, M. J. (1976) Criminal Victimization in Eight American Cities. Cambridge, MA: Ballinger.

JOHNSON, R. (1976) Culture and Crisis in Confinement. Lexington, MA: Lexington Books.

KAHANA, E., J. LIANG, G. FELTON, T. FAIRCHILD, and Z. HAREL (1977) "Perspectives of aged on victimization, 'ageism', and their problems in urban society." Gerontologist 17: 121-130.

KARLINGER, F. and E. J. PEDHAZUR (1973) Multiple Regression in Behavioral Research. New York: Holt, Rinehart & Winston.

LAMBORN, L. (1968) "Toward a victim orientation in criminal theory." Rutgers Law Rev. 22: 733-768.

MENDELSOHN, B. (1963) "The origin of the doctrine of victimology." Exerpta Criminologica 3: 329-444.

OLESEN, V. and E. WHITTAKER (1968) The Silent Dialogue: A Study in the Social Psychology of Professional Socialization. San Francisco: Jossey-Bass.

PARSONS, T. (1951) The Social System. New York: Free Press.

ROTTER, J. B. (1966) "Generalized expectancies for internal versus external control of reinforcement." Psychological Monographs 80: 1-28.

RYAN, W. (1971) Balming the Victim. New York: Vintage.

SCHAFER, S. (1976) Introduction to Criminology. Reston: Reston Publishing Co.

——— (1968) The Victim and His Criminal: A Study in Functional Responsibility. New York: Reston.

SCHRAMM, W., J. LYLE, and E. PARKER (1961) Television in the Lives of Our Children. Palo Alto: Sanford Univ. Press.

SMITH, D. L. (1976) "The aftermath of victimization: fear and suspicion," pp. 203-219 in E. Viano (ed.) Victims and Society. Washington, DC: Visage.

THOMAS, D., D. FRANKS, and J. CALONICO (1972) "Role-taking and power in social psychology." Amer. Soc. Rev. 37: 605-614.

THORNTON, R. and P. M. MARDI (1975) "The dynamics of role acquisition." Amer. J. of Sociology 80: 870-885.

TURNER, R. H. (1962) "Role-taking: process versus conformity," pp. 20-40 in A. Rose (ed.) Human Behavior and Social Processes. Boston: Houghton Mifflin.

U.S. Department of Justice, Law Enforcement Assistance Administration (1975) Criminal Victimization Surveys in the Nation's Five Largest Cities. Washington, DC: Government Printing Office.

VON HENTIG, H. (1948) The Criminal and his Victim. New Haven, CT: Yale Univ. Press.

WOLFGANG, M. (1958) Patterns in Criminal Homicide. Philadelphia: Univ. of Pennsylvania Press.

Vernetta D. Young
American University

5

VICTIMS OF FEMALE OFFENDERS

INTRODUCTION

Criminological researchers have devoted considerable attention, during the past three decades, to the study of the victim, his or her role, and the victim-offender relation (Hindelang, 1976). However, much of the previous research was limited in that: (a) only official sources of data were employed; (b) only the more serious offenses (homicide and aggravated assault) were examined; and (c) there were no comparisons of findings by sex of the offender. In addition, the concern was primarily with the interpersonal relationship of the victim and the offender.

At the same time, researchers who were concerned that offenses known to the police and the courts were not representative of actual crime, introduced two approaches, self-report and victim surveys, to address the issue of "hidden" crime. Victim surveys, the data source used in this report, ask individuals to report incidents of crime for which they have been victims. This approach provides information on criminal activities that is independent of both official sources and of the offender.

AUTHOR'S NOTE: *This is a revised version of a paper presented at the American Society of Criminology (1978). Portions of this essay are drawn from research supported by Grant 75-SS-99-6029 awarded to the Criminal Justice Research Center, Albany, N.Y., by the Statistics Division, National Criminal Justice Information and Statistics Service, Law Enforcement Assistance Administration, U.S. Department of Justice. Points of view or opinions are those of the author and do not necessarily represent the official position of the U.S. Department of Justice.*

72

Because of recent interest in female crime and findings which question assumed differences in female and male criminality, there is a need to reconsider questions relating to the pattern of female criminality. One such question is "Who does the female offender victimize?" This essay will use and alternative source of data—victim surveys—which includes a range of offenses, to examine the relation between the female offender and her victim. The sex, age, race, and interpersonal relation of the victims of female offenders will be examined. The intraage and intraracial nature of the victimizations involving female offenders will also be examined. The results will be compared with the characteristics of the victims of female offenders reported in other sources, and with characteristics of victims of male offenders.

NATIONAL CRIME SURVEY

Under the auspices of the Law Enforcement Assistance Administration (LEAA), the Bureau of the Census conducts the National Crime Survey (NCS). Begun in 1972, it is composed of both a national panel survey and a number of city surveys. The data to be used in this research are derived from the city surveys. Between 1972 and 1975, 26 of the nation's largest cities were surveyed, and a stratified probability of households was drawn.

Residents were asked to report personal and household victimizations suffered by household members age 12 or older during the 12 months preceding the interview. This report will deal only with the personal victimizations (i.e., assaultive violence with theft, assaultive violence without theft, and personal theft without injury). Demographic information about the household and the respondent (age, race, sex, education, and family income), a series of individual screen questions designed to discover whether any of the survey crimes had occurred during the preceding 12 months, and (when the preceding was answered affirmatively) detailed questions about the victimization including offender characteristics (age, race, sex, education, family income) and incident characteristics (time, place, and so forth) were the three major portions of the survey instrument for personal and household respondents.

CHARACTERISTICS OF VICTIMS
OF FEMALE OFFENDERS

Sex of Victim

The data indicated that the victims of female offenders were usually female. This was the case in victimizations committed both by lone female offenders (78%) and multiple female offender groups (88%). These findings differ considerably for male offenders: Lone male offenders were as likely to victimize males as they were to victimize females; multiple male offender groups were more than twice as likely to victimize males (69%) as they were to victimize females (31%).

When examining the influence of the type of crime on the sex of the victims of female offenders, the only suggestions from previous literature come from Bensing and Schroeder (1960), Wolfgang (1958), and Mulvihill et al. (1968). They found for homicide, assault, and armed robbery cases, that female offenders more often killed, assaulted, or robbed male victims than female victims. Although the victim survey data excluded the offense of homicide, assaults and thefts (both serious and minor), were included. Previous studies suggest that for assaultive offenses and for serious theft offenses the victims of female offenders were more often male than female. But this was not the case. The pattern of victim selection for female offenders was not affected by the nature of the offense. In all offense categories, the victims of female offenders were more often female than male.

A closer look at the breakdown of offenses indicates that female offenders tend to victimize males more often for aggravated assault victimizations (close to one-third), than for any other kind of victimization (data now shown). In addition, 25% of all robbery victimizations committed by female offenders involved male victims.

On the other hand, while the pattern of victim selection for multiple male offender groups was stable across offense categories, such was not the case for lone male offenders. For assaultive violence with theft and personal theft without injury, female victims predominated (63% and 59%), but for assaultive violence without theft, male victims predominated (56%).

Age of Victim

For victimizations committed by both lone and multiple female offenders, the rate of victimization decreases as the age of the victim increases. But there is a recognizable difference in the pattern evidenced by the two groups. The rate of victimization for victims of multiple female offenders decreases much more sharply as the age of the victim increases than does the rate for victims of lone female offenders. For both groups of female offenders, lone and multiple, the rate of victimization for victims peaks in the 12 through 15 age group. For every age group, except the youngest, the rate for victims of lone offenders is greater than that for multiple offenders. The greatest difference in victimization rates for victims of lone and multiple offenders is evident for victims between 20- and 34-years-old. The victimization rate for victims of lone offenders who are in this age range is more than 3 times the rate for victims of multiple offenders in this age range.

The difference in the pattern of victimization by age of victim for lone and multiple offenders is much less dramatic than that evidenced for victims of lone and multiple female offenders. For lone male offenders, the rate of victimization increases sharply as age increases from 12 through 15 to 20 through 24 and decreases sharply thereafter. However, the rate for victims of multiple male offenders increases slightly as age increases from 12 through 15, to 16 through 19 and decreases steadily thereafter. Victims of lone and multiple male offenders differ in the age category evidencing the greatest risk of personal victimization with victims of lone male offenders (20-24) somewhat older than victims of multiple male offenders (16-19). In either case (lone or multiple victimizations), victims of male offenders are older than victims of female offenders.

The overall pattern of victimization by age of victim for female offenders, lone and multiple, largely results from the effect of the pattern for assaultive violence without theft. On the contrary, in the case of personal theft without injury, the rate of victimization decreases as age increases from 12 through 19 to 20 through 34 but increases for the 35 and older age group.[1]

There was very little difference in the rate of victimization for older victims (35 and older) of lone female offenders by the type of offense. But for younger victims, between 12 and 34 years old for lone offender victimizations and between 12 and 19 for multiple offender victimizations, the rate of assaultive violence without theft is much greater than the rate of personal theft without injury. In general, younger victims suffered a much greater risk of assault victimization than of theft victimization at the hands of female offenders. In addition, younger victims evidenced a high risk of victimization by both lone and multiple female offenders, whereas older victims evidenced a much higher rate of victimization from lone offenders than from multiple offenders.

Unlike the pattern of victimization by age of victim for lone male offenders, the pattern for multiple male offenders differs by type of offense. For assaultive violence without theft, the rate of victimization increases as age increases from 12 to 15 to 16 through 19, and decreases thereafter. On the other hand, the rate decreases steadily as age increases from 12 through 15 to 25 through 34 for both assaultive violence with theft and personal theft without injury. For assault with theft the rate increases for the 35 through 49 and the 50 through 64 age groups and then decreases for the oldest age group, whereas for personal theft without injury the rate continues to decrease for the 35 through 49 age group but increases thereafter.

Victims under 35 suffered a greater risk of assault, those 50 years of age or older suffered a greater risk of theft, and those between 35 and 49 years old were as likely to be victims of assault as of theft in victimizations committed by lone male offenders. In victimizations committed by multiple male offenders, all age groups, except the 16 through 19 age group, evidenced a greater risk of theft than of assault victimizations.

Age of Offender by Age of Victim

The data indicate that the age of the victim of female offenders differs by the type of offense. It is suggested that there is a relationship between the age of the offender, the age of the victim, and the type of offense. Two hypotheses, advanced by Hindelang (1976), are addressed:

(1) Victims and offenders of assaultive violence without theft victimization will be close to the same age [Hindelang, 1967: 174];

(2) Victims and offenders of personal theft without injury should show more difference in age than do victims and offenders of assaultive violence without theft [Hindelang, 1976: 174].

Of all the variables pertaining to the characteristics of the offender, age is probably most error ridden. Victims were asked to estimate the age(s) of the offender(s). It is expected that there is a margin of error in the accuracy of the victm's perception of the offender's age. For lone and multiple offenders, the perceived ages were categorized as follows: under 12, 12 through 14, 15 through 17, 18 through 20, and 21 or over. For offenders under 21, the concern is the difficulty of discerning the age when categories are so finely differentiated, whereas for offenders over 20 the lack of differentiation between age categories is a source of concern. Because it is impossible to quantify this error, it is important that findings about the age of offenders be scrutinized carefully.

The relationship between the age of the victim and the offender can be examined in two ways. First, if is assumed that there is a high association between the age of the victim and the offender, the main diagonal[2] (from upper left to lower right) will contain a majority of cases (see Table 1). This is true for lone female offenders with the exception of the 18 through 20-year victim-offender group. However, for multiple female offenders this is not the case. Only for the 12 through 14 and the over 20-year-old victims and offenders does the main diagonal contain a majority of cases. For male offenders this pattern (the main diagonal containing a majority of cases) applies only to the over 20-year-old victims and offenders. In the discussion of the intraage group nature of offenses, those offenders reported to be over 20 and their respective victims have been excluded.[3] The data show a greater occurance of peer to peer incidents involving lone female offenders under 17-years-old than any of the other offender groups.

When gamma, a measure of association, is applied to the data, the strength of the relation between the age of lone female offenders and their victims is greater (gamma = .78) than that for multiple female offenders (gamma = .66) and lone and multiple male offenders (gamma = .65 and .63).[4]

Of particular interest is the fact that, for male offenders (lone and multiple), victims over 20 generally constitute the largest proportion of the victims of all offenders regardless of the offender's age. This is not generally true for female offenders. On the contrary, victims over 20 constituted the largest proportion of the victims of lone female offenders (68%), but only 44% of the victims of multiple female offenders.

Examining the type of offense provides the opportunity to address the hypotheses discussed above. As the main diagonals in Table 1 demonstrate, victims and offenders of assaultive violence without theft were reported to be close in age more often than were victims and offenders of personal theft without injury. Victims and offenders of multiple offender groups were more often reported to be under 18 (over 60%). These data generally seem to support the first hypothesis (that the ages of victims and offenders of assaultive violence without theft victimizations would be close), but a more reliable method of determining the

TABLE 1

Age Distribution of Victims by Age of Offender(s) and Type of Crime

| | Age of Victim | | | | | | | | | |
| | Victims of Lone Female Offenders | | | | | Victims of Multiple Female Offenders | | | | |
Type of Crime and Age of Offender(s)[a]	12-14	15-17	18-20	21+	Total	12-14	15-17	18-20	21+	Total
Assaultive Violence Without Theft										
12-14	66%[b]	13%	2%	20%	(9,798) 12%[c]	53%	31%	3%	13%	(11,285) 38%
15-17	24%	49%	7%	20%	(13,175) 17%	18%	47%	19%	16%	(11,874) 40%
18-20	2%	19%	25%	54%	(6,730) 9%	4%	11%	24%	61%	(2,974)[d] 10%
21+	5%	5%	7%	84%	(48,841) 62%	13%	7%	9%	71%	(3,377)[d] 11%
Total	15%	14%	8%	62%	(78,544) 100%	30%	33%	12%	26%	(29,510) 100%
Personal Theft Without Injury										
12-14	47%	10%	10%	33%	(2,934)[d] 10%	35%	36%	2%	27%	(5,101) 23%
15-17	9%	24%	9%	58%	(4,356) 15%	24%	16%	8%	52%	(8,419) 38%
18-20	1%	18%	7%	74%	(3,962) 13%	0%	1%	5%	94%	(3,997) 18%
21+	0%	1%	4%	95%	(18,194) 62%	0%	0%	0%	100%	(4,785) 21%
Total	6%	8%	6%	80%	(29,446) 100%	17%	14%	5%	64%	(22,302) 100%

Table 1 (Continued):

Type of Crime and Age of Offender(s)[a]	Age of Victim									
	Victims of Lone Female Offenders					Victims of Multiple Female Offenders				
	12-14	15-17	18-20	21+	Total	12-14	15-17	18-20	21+	Total
Total Personal Victimization[e]										
12-14	61%	13%	3%	23%	(12,982)	46%	32%	2%	19%	(8,264)
15-17	19%	41%	7%	33%	(19,110)	21%	33%	14%	32%	(22,576)
18-20	2%	17%	17%	64%	(11,698)	2%	5%	11%	82%	(8,165)
21+	4%	4%	6%	87%	(69,373)	5%	4%	3%	87%	(8,742)

Gamma: Female Offenders
Age of lone offender and victim = .78
Age of multiple offender and victim = .66

Male offenders[f]
Age of lone offender and victim = .65
Age of multiple offender and victim = .63

a. Age of the youngest multiple offender in the group.

b. Row percentages.

c. Column percentages.

d. Estimate based on about 50 or fewer sample cases.

e. Assaultive violence with theft victimizations are included in the total.

f. Data for male offenders and mixed-sex group offenders not shown.

age of the offender is necessary before any firm conclusions can be reached.

There is also support for the hypothesis that victims and offenders of personal theft without injury differ more in age than victims and offenders of assaultive violence without theft. There is less difference in the ages of victims and offenders for lone than for multiple victimizations. Still, 80% of the victims of lone female offenders reported being over 20, whereas the offenders were reported to be over 20 in 62% of the victimizations. Victims of multiple female offenders were over 20 in 64% of the victimizations, whereas offenders were most often between 15 and 20 (56%).

In summary, lone female offenders and their victims were usually older than multiple female offenders and their victims. Specifically, the data suggest that lone offender victimizations involve peer to peer incidents for both the junior and senior high school age groups (12 through 17), whereas for multiple offender victimizations the peer to peer incidents mainly involve the junior high school age group (12 through 14).

Race of the Victim

The victims of female and male offenders, lone and multiple, tend overwhelmingly to be white (about 67%). However, the rate of victimization for victims of female offenders differs little by race; for black victims the rate was 9 per 1,000, while for white and other victims the rates were 8 and 7. For male offenders, there is considerably more difference by race of victim, with black victims evidencing a much higher rate (137) than either white (103) or other victims (64). Across offense categories, the rate of victimization for victims of female offenders differs little by race of the victim. However, for victims of male offenders there is more difference in the rate of victimization by race of the victim for theft offenses (assaultive violence with theft and personal theft without injury) than for purely assault offenses (assaultive violence without theft).

Previous studies of the victim-offender relation have reported that most crime is intraracial (Wolfgang, 1958; Mulvihill et al., 1968). In the next section we will examine the stability of this relation by the sex of the offender and type of victimization.

RACE OF OFFENDER BY RACE OF VICTIM

Over the last decade, issues of racism and sexism have received widespread attention. Laws dealing with discrimination have been enacted at both federal and state levels. But American society remains, in most respects, racially segregated (housing, social relationships, and so forth). In addition, women are still restricted, especially in social relations, by traditional sexual-role prescriptions. Because female behavior is more circumscribed, it seems more likely that women are more racially segregated than men. Therefore, it is hypothesized that female offenders and their victims are more often members of the same race than are male offenders and their victims.

It appears from our data that the sex of the offender has little to do with the intraracial nature of the victim-offender interaction. Regardless of the offender's sex, for both lone and multiple victimizations, white offenders victimized whites in almost 90% of the total cases. These same results were evident for other offenders. In lone offender victimizations, regardless of sex, black offenders were as likely to victimize whites as blacks, but in multiple offender victimizations, black offender groups—female and male—were more likely to victimize whites than blacks. This finding is more outstanding for female offender groups (60%) than for male offender groups (53%).

When the type of offense is examined (assaultive violence without theft and personal theft without injury), white offenders (lone and multiple, female and male) more often victimized whites than blacks or others, whereas for black offenders the pattern of victim selection differs by offense type and group context (lone and multiple). For lone offender victimizations, regardless of sex, black offenders victimized whites more often than blacks or others in personal theft without injury victimizations, whereas in assaultive violence without theft victimizations, black offenders were more likely to victimize whites than to victimize blacks or others.

Another way of assessing the intraracial nature of victimizations is to examine the victim-offender racial dyads. There is no difference in the proportion of intraracial victimizations by sex of the offender in lone offender victimizations. Almost two-thirds of all lone offender victimizations were intraracial. On the other hand, multiple male offender groups were involved in intraracial victimizations slightly more often (54%) than were multiple female offender groups (47%). Assaultive violence without theft victimizations was more likely to be intraracial than was personal theft without injury victimizations, regardless of whether the offenders were male or female, or the victimization involved lone or multiple offenders. One interesting difference is that personal theft without injury victimizations by female offender groups were less likely to be intraracial (35%) than those by either male offender groups or lone offenders, female or male (close to 50% for each).

Interpersonal Relationship

Since Lombroso, the interpersonal relation between the female offender and her victim has received considerably more attention than other aspects of the victim-offender relation. Some studies (Lombroso, 1903; Pollak, 1950; Wolfgang, 1958) concluded that female offenders more often victimized either the men in their lives (husbands or lovers) or members of their immediate families (children, siblings, and parents). Explanations for this finding have been based on assumptions about the female role as wife and mother. Most of these works have dealt with violent crimes such as homicide and assault.

There is one limitation of the victim survey data relating to the interpersonal relation between victims and offenders that must be recognized. Interviews with victims selected from police files in Washington, D.C. (U.S. Bureau of the Census, 1970a), Baltimore (U.S. Bureau of the Census,

1970b), and San Jose, California (LEAA, 1972), indicated that reporting problems were especially acute for assault offenses. Furthermore, the results of the San Jose Reverse Record Check Study (LEAA, 1972) indicated that those assaultive offenses which involved an offender related to the victim were less likely to be reported to the interviewer (22%) than those involving either an offender known to the victim but not a relative (55%) or a stranger (54%). Accurate measurement of these types of offenses was therefore difficult.[5] However, there is no evidence to suggest that the problem is any more acute for females than for males.

The data indicate that lone female offenders were more often nonstrangers (56%) than strangers to their victims; multiple female offender groups were more often strangers (63%). For male offenders, this change in pattern by type of offender group *does not occur.* Instead, both types of offender are more apt to be strangers to their victims, although there was a degree of difference—lone male offenders victimize strangers less often (67%) than do multiple male offenders (85%).

Two important changes in the pattern of interpersonal victim-offender relationships are evident when the nature of the offenses is considered. First, contrary to the overall pattern, lone female offenders committing personal theft without injury more often victimized strangers (79%) than nonstrangers. This can be attributed to the nature of the offenses committed by females in this category, namely purse snatching and pocket picking (data not shown). In the case of assaultive violence without theft, lone female offenders more often victimized nonstrangers (70%); on the other hand, for both assaultive violence without theft (53%) and personal theft without injury (87%), lone male offenders were more often strangers to their victims. Second, multiple female offenders committing assaultive violence without theft, victimized nonstrangers in 55% of the victimizations compared with multiple male offenders who victimized nonstrangers in only 24% of their assaultive violence without theft victimizations. For personal theft without injury, strangers were victimized in 87% of the victimizations committed by multiple female offenders and 90% of those committed by multiple male offenders.

A closer look at the victim-offender relation indicates that although the majority of well-known victims were not relatives, the victims of lone male offenders were more often relatives (32%) than were victims of lone female offenders (21%). Victims of group offenders rarely reported victimization by relatives.

SUMMARY

The purpose of this essay was to examine the relation between the female offender and her victim. Briefly, the victims of female offenders were young (12-15) females. The rate of victimization differed little by the race of the victim. Finally, victims of lone offender victimizations were more often nonstrangers, whereas victims of multiple offender victimizations were usually strangers.

All the characteristics of the victims of female offenders, except the sex of the victim, differed across offense categories. In assaultive violence without theft victimizations the victims of female offenders were generally young and nonstrangers (in multiple offender victimizations), whereas in personal theft without injury, victims were older and strangers (in lone offender victimizations). The race of the victims of female offenders in assaultive violence without theft (lone offender victimizations) was more often black but usually in interaction with a black offender (see below).

On the other hand, the victims of male offenders were usually young (16-24), black, male strangers. At this point it seems clear that females do not follow the same patterns of victimizing as males. Female and male offenders differed in each of the variables examined. Furthermore, all the characteristics of the victims of male offenders, except the interpersonal victim-offender relationship, differed for lone and multiple offender victimizations and across offense categories.

The intra-age and intraracial nature of victimizations involving female offenders was examined in light of previous studies. Hindelang (1976: 174) reported that in purely assaultive offenses, victims and offenders would be close to the same age, whereas in theft offenses there would be a greater difference in the ages of victims and offenders. Both hypotheses were supported for female offenders and their victims.

The intraracial nature of crime has also been noted in the literature (Wolfgang, 1958: Mulvihill et al., 1969). Victimizations involving female offenders were about as likely to be intraracial as those involving male offenders. It seems that the sex of the offender had little influence.

Finally, the data indicate that the victims of female offenders were more often nonstrangers than were the victims of male offenders. This difference was especially salient for lone offender assaultive violence without theft victimizations. Although the victims of female offenders were more often nonstrangers than were the victims of male offenders they were less likely to be relatives if the offender was female than if the offender was male. The data presented provide partial support for earlier findings. However, it is evident that the nature of the victimization is very important in discussing differences in the interpersonal victim-offender relation of female and male offenders.

Overall, these findings suggest that the victim-offender relation of female offenders is sufficiently different from that of male offenders to necessitate independent consideration. It is further suggested that there is a need to study female crime systematically, thereby contributing to a body of knowledge in female crime which addresses both the differences among female offenders and between female and male offenders.

NOTES

1. Age categories were regrouped (12-19, 20-34, 35 and over) so that a sufficient number of victimizations, by type of offense and sex of victim, were included for a statistically reliable estimate. Assaultive violence with theft victimizations are

excluded from most of the analysis because in making comparisons of victims of female offenders by age and race there are not a sufficient number of cases for statistically reliable estimates.

2. The main diagonal refers to same age offenders and victims. For example, the intersection of offenders from age 12 through 14 with victims from age 12 through 14 is the starting point for the main diagonal.

3. Victims and offenders over 20 were excluded from the discussion of the intragroup nature of offenses because the lack of differentiation between age categories for over 20 offenders makes it impossible to compare these groups with a same age victim group.

4. Gamma is a measure of association for ordinal variables based on the difference between ranks. Its value ranges from $+1.0$ to -1.0. Victims and offenders over 20 were excluded from the calculations (see note 4). Also excluded were offenders under 12 because of their small numbers.

5. Hindelang (1976: 63, 75) points out that in Table 1 of LEAA's (1972) publication there is an error in the reported proportion of police sample cases of assault involving an offender known to the victim.

REFERENCES

BENSING, R. C., and O. J. SCHROEDER (1960) Homicide in an Urban Community. Springfield, IL: Charles C Thomas.

HINDELANG, M. J. (1976) Criminal Victimization in Eight American Cities: A Descriptive Analysis of Common Theft and Assault. Cambridge, MA: Ballinger.

——, M. GOTTFREDSON, and J. GAROFALO (1978) Victims of Personal Crime: An Empirical Foundation for a Theory of Personal Victimization. Cambridge, MA: Ballinger.

Law Enforcement Assistance Administration (1972) San Jose Methods Test of Known Crime Victims. Washington, DC: Government Printing Office.

LOMBROSA, C. (1903) The Female Offender. New York: Philosophical Library.

MULVIHILL, D., M. TUMIN, and L. CURTIS (1969) Crimes of Violence, Vol. II: A Staff Report Submitted to the National Commission on the Causes and Prevention of Violence. Washington, DC: Government Printing Office.

POLLAK, O. (1950) The Criminality of Women. Philadelphia: Univ. of Pennsylvania Press.

United States Bureau of the Census (1970a) "Victim recall pretest (Washington, D.C.): Household survey of victims of crime." Suitland, MD.: U.S. Bureau of the Census, Demographic Surveys Division (mimeo).

—— (1970b) "Household survey of victims of crime: Second pretest (Baltimore, (Md.) Suitland, MD: U.S. Bureau of the Census, Demographic Surveys Division. (mimeo).

David L. Decker
Robert M. O'Brien
David Shichor
California State College, San Bernardino

6

PATTERNS OF JUVENILE VICTIMIZATION AND URBAN STRUCTURE

There is an increasing volume of criminological literature dealing with juvenile delinquency and its correlates. But little attention has been paid to the problem of the criminal victimization of juveniles, with the exception of the recent upsurge of interest in child abuse (Bakan, 1972; Chase, 1975). This is surprising, since victimization surveys show that juveniles consistently report the highest rates of victimization among all age groups. There has been a great deal of concern with the criminal victimization of other age groups, e.g., the victimization of the elderly has received special attention, in part because of the older age group's fear of victimization (see Goldsmith and Goldsmith, 1976; O'Brien et al., 1978). However, Lalli and Savitz (1976) found that there are also high levels of fear of victimization among juveniles. Because of the high rates of victimization, as well as the apparent fear, it seems appropriate to attend to the subject of juvenile victimization.

To a certain extent the arrest rates and the victimization rates of various age groups tend to be parallel. For example, Empey (1978) points out that the victimization rate for personal crimes (rape, robbery, assault, and larceny) decreases with each older age group after adolescence, just as do the arrest rates. The pattern for violent crimes is different for juveniles, because even though juveniles do not have the highest arrest rate for these crimes, they are the ones most likely to be victimized. Thus the correlates of crime rates and victimization rates for juveniles are not necessarily the same. In this paper we will examine the victimization rates of juveniles.

There is research which has investigated the relation between the urban structure and the types and rates of juvenile delinquency. For example, the Chicago School has delineated the concentration of juvenile delinquency in specific parts of large urban areas (Shaw and McKay, 1969). It is also known that most criminal offenders and their victims reside in those parts of urban areas where there is a high concentration of low income groups, such as the elderly and ethnic minorities (Wilson, 1970). Therefore, a comparative study of the urban characteristics associated with juvenile victimization seems to be an appropriate starting point in this neglected area. This essay investigates the relation between juvenile victimization and the urban structure for 26 central cities of the United States.

PROCEDURES

This study examines the relation among several urban structural characteristics and National Crime Survey victimization rates (NCS rates) for juveniles (ages 12 to 19 in 26 large American central cities.[1] These victimization surveys include rates for: property crimes without contact (household larceny, household burglary, personal larceny without contact, and motor vehicle theft); nonproperty assaultive crimes (simple assault, aggravated assault, and rape); and property crimes with contact (robbery with injury, robbery without injury, and personal larceny with contact).

The major problem in the analysis was to determine which structural characteristics of cities to examine. This problem was exacerbated by the fact that there are only 26 cities included in the surveys.[2] We followed three rules in the selection of independent variables: (1) We selected those shown in previous studies to be related to crime rates;[3] (2) We attempted to use a single measure as an indicator for similar characteristics whenever possible;[4] and (3) We attempted to combine independent variables which are closely related both theoretically and statistically.[5] The independent variables for the study are: population density (population per square mile), percentage of the population between 12 and 19 years of age, percentage white, percentage foreign born, percentage unemployed, percentage on public assistance, percentage blue collar, and a summative index based on the median income and education for each city (SEI, socio-economic index).[6]

Stepwise multiple regression was used to assess the relation of each of the structural characteristics to the rate of juvenile victimization. This allowed us to evaluate whether each new variable entering the regression equation accounted for additional (unaccounted for) variance in the dependent variable. Our strategy regressed each victimization rate (dependent variable) on the urban structure characteristics (independent variables) for all 26 cities. We then assessed the statistical significance of the additional contribution of each new independent variable using an F-test.[7]

RESULTS

The results of the stepwise multiple regression for juvenile victimization by property crimes without contact are summarized in Table 1. The most consistent result was that density is the first variable to enter each of these equations. The proportion of intercity variation accounted for by density ranges from 64% for household larceny to 21% for motor vehicle theft. The relation among density and the rates of household larceny, burglary, and personal larceny without contact are statistically significant at the .001 level. The relation between density and motor vehicle theft is significant at the .05 level. Each of the property crimes without contact is negatively related to population density. That is to say, those cities which are less densely populated tend to have a higher rate of juvenile victimization for these four crimes. Another important urban structural characteristic accounting for intercity variation is the percentage of white

TABLE 1
Stepwise Regression for Property Crimes Without Contact[†]

	R^2	Change in R^2	F-Value for Change in R^2	Zero-Order r
Dependent Variable: *Household Burglary*				
Density	.42	.42	17.54****	−.65
Dependent Variable: *Household Larcency*				
Density	.64	.64	42.96****	−.80
Percentage White	.76	.12	11.56***	.50
Dependent Variable: *Motor Vehicle Theft*				
Density	.21	.21	6.20**	−.45
SEI	.32	.11	3.69*	.42
Dependent Variable: *Personal Larcency Without Contact*				
Density	.52	.52	26.21****	−.72
Percentage White	.75	.23	21.21****	.61
SEI	.84	.09	11.89***	.60
Percentage Foreign Born	.87	.03	4.47**	−.36

[†]This table includes only those independent variables which are significantly related to juvenile victimization ($p < .10$).
 *Change in R square is significant at the .10 level.
 **Change in R square is significant at the .05 level.
 ***Change in R square is significant at the .01 level.
 ****Change in R square is significant at the .001 level.

population in the city. This variable is positively related to both household larceny and personal larceny without contact. The percentage of white population accounts for an additional 12% of the variation in household larceny ($p < .01$) and an additional 13% ($p < .001$) of the variation in personal larceny without contact.

An additional variable which has some explanatory power is the socioeconomic index (SEI; see n. 6). It contributes an additional 9% to the explained variance in personal larceny without contact ($p < .01$), and an additional 11% to the explained variance in motor vehicle theft (albeit $p > .05$ but p < .10). This variable is positively related to both of these rates. The final structural characteristic which adds significantly to the explained variance of these victimization rates is the percentage of foreign born people in the city. This variable adds 3% (p < .05) to the explained variance in personal larceny without contact.

The urban structural characteristics employed in the analysis account for an unusually large proportion of the variation in victimizations by household larceny and personal larceny without contact. Four urban structural characteristics account for 87% of the variation in juvenile victimization by personal larceny without contact, while two sructural characteristics account for 76% of the variation in household larceny victimization.

Table 2 presents the results of our stepwise analysis for nonproperty assaultive crimes (rape, simple assault, and aggravated assault). The most consistent findings for these rates of juvenile victimization were that the percentage of whites in urban areas was the first variable to enter each of the equations. The proportion of intercity variation accounted for by the percentage of whites varied from 22% for rape and aggravated assault (p < .05) to 41% for simple assault (p < .001). The relation between the percentage of white and juvenile victimization is positive for each type of crime. That is, those cities with a higher percentage of white population tend to have a higher rate of juvenile victimization by nonproperty assaultive crimes.

Another important structural characteristic which accounted for additional variation in these victimization rates was the percentage of the foreign born urban population. This structural characteristic contributes 28% to the variation accounted for in juvenile victimization by aggravated assault (p < .01), 17% to the variation accounted for in victimization by simple assault (p < .01), and 10% to the variation in victimization by forcible rape (p < .01). The relation between the percentage foreign born and these victimization rates was negative. That is, cities with a higher percentage of foreign born tend to have lower rates of victimization for these crimes.

TABLE 2
Stepwise Regression or Nonproperty Assaultive Crimes[†]

	R^2	Change in R^2	F-Valued for Change in R^2	Zero-Order r
Dependent Variable: *Rape*				
Percentage White	.22	.22	6.64**	.47
Percentage Unemployed	.31	.10	3.23*	.33
Percentage Foreign Born	.42	.11	4.08*	−.21
Percentage 12 to 19	.50	.08	3.34*	−.20
Dependent Variable: *Aggravate Assault*				
Percentage White	.22	.22	6.67**	.47
Percentage Foreign Born	.49	.28	12.48***	−.44
Dependent Variable: *Simple Assault*				
Percentage White	.41	.41	16.61****	.64
Percentage Foreign Born	.58	.17	9.54***	−.31
Percentage Unemployed	.69	.11	7.45**	.31
Percentage Blue Collar	.73	.04	3.07*	−.33

[†]This table includes only those independent variables which are significantly related to juvenile victimization ($p < .10$).
*Change in R square is significant at the .10 level.
**Change in R square is significant at the .05 level.
***Change in R square is significant at the .01 level.
****Change in R square is significant at the .001 level.

Percentage unemployed adds significantly to the explained variance of two types of victimization: forcible rape and simple assault. It adds 11% to the variance accounted for in simple assault ($p < .05$), and 10% to the variance accounted for in forcible rape ($0 < .10$). For both of these types of victimization, the greater the percentage unemployed the greater the victimization rate. Two other variables contributed modestly to the explained variance, but neither was statistically significant at the .05 level (these variables were the percentage blue collar and the percentage of the population between 12 and 19 years of age, both of which were negatively correlated with juvenile victimization).

The analysis showed that 73% of the intercity variation in juvenile victimization by simple assault was accounted for by four structural characteristics of urban areas (percentage white, percentage foreign born, percentage unemployed, and percentage blue collar). In the case of juvenile victimization by forcible rape, 50% of the variance was explained by four structural characteristics (percentage, white, percentage unemployed, percentage foreign born, and percentage of population in the age group 12 to 19 years). Finally in the case of juvenile victimization by aggravated assault, two urban structural variables accounted for 49% of the variance (percentage white and percentage foreign born).

The stepwise regression analysis for property crimes with contact (personal larceny with contact, robbery without injury and robbery with injury) indicated that the structural characteristics of cities used in our analysis were not very useful in accounting for variance in these crimes. The only structural characteristic which entered any of the equations for these three crimes is SEI, which accounted for only 16% of the intercity variation in personal larceny without contact.

DISCUSSION

In examining the structural characteristics which account for intercity variation in the victimization rates of juveniles for property crimes without contact, one is impressed by the consistently high negative relation between victimization rates and density, and the fact that the relation is negative is especially interesting in light of the supposedly positive relationship between crime and density (see Shaw and McKay, 1969; Mladenka and Hill, 1976; Wirth, 1938).[8] Given the fact that the data we are analyzing are on the city-level of analysis, it is not possible to provide a definitive explanation of this relationship. However, we can speculate that in cities which are more densely populated it is more difficult to commit property crimes without contact because of an increase in visibility under the condition of high density. This fact has been noted by Cunningham (1976) and Reppetto (1974). Cunningham (1976: 47-48) states that the burglar "actively attempts to avoid human contact. He is thus more than usually sensitive to evidence of occupancy, of being observed and possibly reported out of suspicion, and being surprised in the process of his crime." Reppetto (1974: 16) finds in his interviews with adjudicated burglars that they seek out isolated neighborhoods where they feel inconspicuous.

A consistent pattern also emerged from the analysis of the structural characteristics which account for intercity variations in nonproperty assaultive crimes. For all three of these crimes (simple assault, aggravated assault, and rape), the percentage white and the percentage foreign born entered the equations. In each case the higher the percentage of the population that is white and the lower the percentage that is foreign born, the higher the rates of victimization.

Although this pattern is consistent for all three types of nonproperty assaultive crimes, our explanation of the pattern remains very tentative. First, what constitutes an assaultive crime is problematic and especially so for juveniles. Sellin and Wolfgang (1964: 83) note that street fights, domestic quarrels, and scuffles at schools are often considered by juveniles to be assaults, even though they are not considered to be felonious assaults. Second, although these results might indicate that whites and "non-foreign born" have higher rates of nonproperty assaultive victimization, this is clearly not the case. For example, the 1976 victimization survey (U.S. Department of Justice, 1976c: 15) indicates that the rape victimization rate for whites was .7 (per 1000) while it was 1.9 for blacks; the assault victimization rate of whites was 24.9 and for blacks 28.9. Thus we see that blacks have a higher victimization rate for these crimes than whites. As is well known, the results of aggregate analysis must be carefully interpreted, i.e., the relation between the percentage of the population which is white and the rate of nonproperty assaultive crimes indicates only that cities with a higher percentage of white citizens tend to have higher rates of victimization by nonproperty assaultive crimes. Third, one might even speculate that the higher percentage of whites provides a larger pool of victims for non-white criminals. This argument is contradicted by a number of studies which indicate that non-property assaultive crimes tend to be intraracial rather than interracial (see Amir, 1971; Curtis, 1975; and Wolfgang, 1958).

CONCLUSION

In this article we have examined the urban structural characteristics associated with intercity variation in juvenile victimization rates. This is a neglected area of research, since much of the literature has concerned juveniles as offenders rather than victims, and has not attempted to account for intercity variation in victimization rates.

The analysis discovered an unexpected relation between population density and property crimes without contact. There is a strong negative relation among motor vehicle theft, household larceny and household burglary, and population density. We have suggested that this may be due to the increased "visibility" which occurs under the condition of high population density.

Although we have not been able to provide a satisfactory explanation of the pattern of intercity variation for non-property assaultive victimization of juveniles, the pattern of intercity variation is clear (i.e., victimization tends to be greater in those cities with a higher percentage of white population and a lower percentage of foreign born).

The approach used in this study has proven to be of some value. Strong relationships were obtained using urban structural characteristics as independent variables in accounting for juvenile victimization by property crimes without contact and non-property assaultive crimes. However, this approach has been less useful in accounting for property crimes with contact. Further investigations of the patterns discovered are needed, and the reasons for the differences in the effect of the structural variables on the different types of crime should be explored.

NOTES

1. We included all of the cities surveyed in the National Crime Survey (U.S. Department of Justice, 1975; 1976a; 1976b). To examine victimization rates for the age group 12-19 for robbery with injury, robbery without injury, aggravated assault, simple assault, personal larceny with contact, and personal larceny without contact, it was necessary to combine the victimization rates for the 12-15 and 16-19 age groups. This was accomplished by multiplying the number of residents in each of the two age groups by the rate for that age group, and adding these products together. This sum was then divided by the total number for the two age groups.

2. The limited number of cities creates a statistical problem when employing multiple regression analysis. If we include too many independent variables, a large part of the variance in victimization rates accounted for by the structural characteristics of cities may be due to "chance fitting."

3. For a discussion of the independent variables employed in our research, see the following sources: Booth et al. (1976); Clinard (1968); Shichor, et al., (1979); Cressy (1966); and Wolfgang (1970).

4. For example, we used percent blue collar as a "stand in" for other possible measures of the occupational structure that were available, i.e., percentage of professionals and percentage of white collar. The correlations between these measures and percentage of blue collar are over .95.

5. Our measure of socioeconomic conditions was based on both the median income and median education for each city. The correlation for these two variables was .71.

6. Data on the independent variables were obtained from the 1970 census (U.S. Bureau of the Census, 1976). Our measure of socioeconomic conditions (SEI) was computed by using the z-scores for median income and median education and then summing these z-scores for each city.

7. The F-test we use is one recommended by Cohen and Cohen (1975: 107, formula 3.7.6, Model 1).

8. On the other hand, several researchers have found a negative relation between population density and victimization rates. See Kvalseth (1975; 1977); Boland (1976); Shichor et al., (1978).

REFERENCES

AMIR, M. (1971) Patterns of Forcible Rape. Chicago: Univ. of Chicago Press.

BAKAN, D. (1972) Slaughter of the Innocents. Boston: Beacon Press.

BOLAND, B. (1976) "Patterns of urban crime," in W. G. Skogan (ed.) Sample Surveys of the Victims of Crime. Cambridge, MA: Ballinger.

BOOTH, A., S. WELCH and, D. R. JOHNSON (1976) "Crowding and urban crime." Urban Affairs Q. 11: 291-307.

CHASE, N. (1975) A Child is Being Beaten. New York: McGraw-Hill.

CLINARD, M. (1968) Sociology of Deviant Behavior. New York: Holt, Rinehart & Winston.

CRESSY, D. R. (1966) "Crime," in R. K. Merton and R. Nisbet (eds.) Contemporary Social Problems. New York: Harcourt, Brace & World.

CUNNINGHAM, C. L. (1976) "Patterns and effect of crime against the aging: the Kansas City study," in J. Goldsmith and S. S. Goldsmith (eds.) Crime and the Elderly. Lexington, MA: D. C. Heath.

CURTIS, L. A. (1975) Violence, Race, and Culture. Lexington, MA: D. C. Heath.

EMPEY, L. T. (1978) American Delinquency: Its Meaning and Construction. Homewood: The Dorsey Press.

GOLDSMITH, J., and S. S. GOLDSMITH [eds.] (1976) Crime and the Elderly. Lexington, MA: D. C. Heath.

KVALSETH, T. O. (1975) "Statistical models of urban crime: a study of burglary." Presented at the Joint National Meeting of the Operations Research Society of America and the Institute of Management Sciences, Las Vegas, Nevada, November 17-19.

——— (1977) "A note on the effects of population density and density in urban crime." Criminology, 15, 1: 105-110.

LALLI, M. and L. D. SAVITZ (1976) "The fear of crime in the school enterprise and its consequences," Education and Urban Society, 8 (August): 401-416.

MLADENKA, K. R. and K. Q. HILL (1976) "A reexamination of the etiology of urban crime." Criminology 13, 4: 491-506.

O'BRIEN, R. M., D SHICHOR, and D. L. DECKER (1978) "Urban structure and household victimization of the eldery." Presented at the 9th World Congress of Sociology, Uppsala, Sweden, August.

REPPETTO, T. A. (1974) Residential Crime. Cambridge, MA: Ballinger.

SELLIN, T. and J. E. WOLFGANG (1964) The Measurement of Delinquency. New York: John Wiley.

SHAW, C. R., and H. D. McKAY (1969) Juvenile Delinquency and Urban Areas (rev. ed). Chicago: Univ. of Chicago Press.

SHICHOR, D., D. L. DECKER, and R. M. O'BRIEN (1979) "An empirical analysis of population density and criminal victimization in central cities: some unexpected findings." Criminology (forthcoming).

U.S. Bureau of the Census (1976) Statistical Abstract of the United States: 1976. Washington, DC: Government Printing Office.

U.S. Department of Justice (1976a) Criminal Victimization Surveys in Eight American Cities. Washington, DC: Government Printing Office.

——— (1976b) Victimization Surveys in Chicago, Detroit, Los Angeles, New York, Philadelphia. Washington, DC: Government Printing Office.

——— (1976c) Criminal Victimization in the United States. Washington, DC: Government Printing Office.

WILSON, J. Q. (1970) "Crime," in D. P. Moynihan (ed.) Toward a National Urban Policy. New York: Basic Books.

WIRTH, L. (1938) "Urbanism as a way of life." Amer. J. of Sociology, 4: 1-24.

WOLFGANG, M. E. (1958) Patterns in Criminal Homicide. Philadelphia: Univ. of Pennsylvania Press.

Samuel D. Smithyman
Human Services Center, Beverly Hills, California

7

CHARACTERISTICS OF "UNDETECTED" RAPISTS

INTRODUCTION

In the United States, rape and sexual violence are growing
social problems. From 1969 to 1976 the rate of reported
rapes per 100,000 inhabitants, as recorded in the Uniform
Crime reports (1977, hereafter cited as UCR), increased
45% while the overall number of rapes reported to law enforcement officials during the same period increased 53%.

Although official statistics on the incidence of reported
rape have shown a dramatic increase, it is not whether this
increase also indicates similar increases in unreported
rapes (UCR, 1977). The uncertainty over whether official
statistics indicate an actual increase in the number of rapes,
an increase in the reporting rate (Mulvihill and Tumin,
1969), or proportionate increases resulting from a growth in
population (Goldner, 1972), reflects how little is known.

Even though law enforcement officials across the country
have recognized rape as one of the most underreported of
all Crime Index Offenses (UCR, 1977), there has been considerable controversy over how to estimate the actual number of rapes that occur. Some feminist writers (e.g., Griffin,
1971; Horos, 1974) have alleged that figures reported in the
UCR should be multiplied by a factor of 10 to obtain an accurate estimate. Survey research conducted by the National

AUTHOR'S NOTE: *Space constraints restrict tabular display of the data.
For more exhaustive quantitative exposition of the material, please con-
tact the author, Human Services Center, 415 N. Camden Drive, Beverly
Hills, Calif. 90212.*

Opinion Research Center (NORC) for the President's Commission on Law Enforcement and Administration of Justice revealed that rape victimization reported among their respondents was almost four times that expected by FBI estimates for rate per 100,000 inhabitants (Mulvihill and Tumin, 1969).

Since according to the UCR (1977) there were 56,730 rapes reported in 1976, use of the NORC survey data showing rape victimization to be approximately four times greater than the figure reported annually to law enforcement agencies would place the "true" number of rapes in the United States in 1976 close to 226,920 (see Figure 1). If, on the other hand, one accepts the feminist position that only one out of ten rapes is reported to police officials, the "true" number of rapes would be closer to 567,300 in 1976. Regardless of the figure, it is clear that the magnitude of the problem is substantially greater than criminal statistics indicate, and that research designed to increase our understanding of the problem will not provide definitive answers to questions about rape and sexual assault in the absence of data from that large population of "undetected" rapes.

More striking than the statistics showing the gap between the reported and the "true" number of rapes are those which bear on an issue variously termed "attrition of justice" or "criminal case mortality" (Rose, 1976). Such phrases refer to the attrition of cases from initial report of victimization through trial and conviction. Figure 1 presents in diagram the "attrition" of rape cases from the criminal justice process for 1974. The UCR does not present data on the sentences that were given to those convicted.

If one combines the number of convictions for rape and the number convicted of some lesser crime (perhaps as a result of plea bargaining) only about 16% of the rapes reported to the police annually lead to some type of conviction. It is even more startling to consider that if one uses the conservative NORC survey finding that only about one out of every four rapes is reported to law enforcement officials, then only about 5% of all rapes lead to some type of conviction in the criminal courts.

Total Rapes in the U.S. (Most conservative estimate) 226,920	(100%) _____
Reported to Law Enforcement 56,730	(25%) _____
Arrests 29,500	(13%) _____
Prosecutions 20,355	(9%) ____
*All convictions 10,381	(5%) ___
Rape convictions 8,549	(4%) __
**Imprisoned for rape (?)	(?)

Figure 1: Attrition of Justice in Rape Cases (1976)
  *Includes convictions for lesser offenses.
  **Further attrition occurs here since only a portion of those convicted receive prison sentences. Unfortunately, the UCR does not present this data.

The implications of this attrition for our understanding of the rapist are clear once it is realized that virtually every systematic investigation of the rapist has employed institutionalized felons as research subjects (e.g., Cohen et al., 1971; Gebhard et al., 1965; Guttmacher, 1951; Karpman, 1954; Queen's Bench Foundation: Rape Preventions and Resistance Study, 1976).

Clearly, some serious limitations must be placed on the generalization of findings from prison populations to the general population of rapists. Prison populations are biased in favor of offenders who do not have the kind of social status or the financial resources to influence judges and prosecutors to use alternatives to penal confinement. In addition to containing a disproportionate number of persons from the lower socioeconomic class, imprisoned rapists are likely to have extensive criminal records in terms of frequency of arrest. It should also be pointed out that imprisoned rapists may also contain a larger proportion of those who have committed violent and brutal rapes. For example, it is unlikely that persons convicted of rape-murder would be found on probation, given a suspended sentence, or acquitted. Given that fewer than 5% of all rapes lead to conviction and that only a portion of those results in prison sentences, findings from research limited to imprisoned rapists are likely to be unrepresentative of rapists in general.

Whether rapists who are caught differ from those who escape detection is an important empirical question bearing on both our understanding of the dynamics of the crime and the men we call "rapists." Without evidence to the contrary, it is plausible that there might be important differences in age, race, education, intelligence, motivation, judgment, and psychopathy between detected and undetected rapists. Similar differences may exist between those apprehended and those not, between those tried and not tried, between those convicted and not convicted, and between those institutionalized and not institutionalized.

The purpose of this research was to begin the systematic investigation of the characteristics and behavior of noninstitutionalized male rapists. The study concerned those males who had raped women but who, for the most part, had managed to avoid contact with the criminal justice system (hence, the "undetected" rapist). Further, the research was begun to explore the dynamics of rape and sexual assault from the perspective of the rapist. It was directed toward increasing our understanding of the factors which influence a man's decision to rape a particular woman and the events which subsequently ensue from that decision. The "undetected" rapists' phenomenological experience of the rape, including his own description of the motivational, strategic, ecological, demographic, and selection boundaries of the event composed the major thrust of the research. Inquiry was guided by a series of specific questions: (1) Who are the "undetected" rapists; (2) What motivates them; (3) Do they plan their attacks, and if so, how do they select their victims; and (4) How has the rape of a woman affected their lives? Only the first of these four questions will be examined. The remainder have been addressed in previous work by the author (Smithyman, 1978).

Several researchers and students of rape (e.g., Amir, 1971; Burgess and Holmstrom, 1974; Connell and Wilson, 1974; Russell, 1975) have recognized the limitations of the research concerning institutionalized rapists. They have been acutely aware of the importance of obtaining good empirical data on rapists from other than institutionalized populations (i.e., data from what Amir termed the "dark figure" of unreported rape). Prior to the current research, however, no one had devised a method of systematically studying that large population of rapists who remain outside the criminal justice system.

METHODOLOGY

Subject Population

The subjects of this research were male rapists who responded to advertisements for their participation in an anonymous telephone interview. The ads were placed in the personals columns of several metropolitan Los Angeles newspapers. The ads read:

Are you a rapist? Researcher interviewing rapists anon. by phone. Identity protected. Phone (213) 553-8996 between 9 a.m. and 9 p.m. Mon — Fri.

The decision to continue the ad in a particular number was based on two criteria: the cost of running the ad, and the number of responses generated. As the study progressed, the Los Angeles *Free Press* became the major source of data.

Research Definition of Rape

The law generally defines rape as sexual intercourse with a female, not the wife of the assailant, accomplished without the consent of the female through the use of force or the threat of force (UCR, 1977).

In this research project, it was decided to concur with the legal definition in some respects, but not in others. Since the use of force and the victim's lack of consent appear to be more important in defining a sexual assault than the type of sexual activity demanded by the perpetrator, rape was defined as "intercourse" imposed on a female against her wishes either by physical force or verbal threats of force. Instances were included where, by virtue of being unconscious, drugged, or being in some comparable state, the women were in no position to consent to the acts demanded by their assailant(s) or to escape from the situation. "Intercourse" implies penetration, but not necessarily vaginal nor by the penis; thus, anal or oral penetration was also regarded as rape, as was penetration by a foreign object. This agreed with the definition of rape used by Russell (1974) in her study of rape victims. Although it was recognized that males may sexually assault other males and that women can assault men, this study examined only those sexual assaults where men were the assailants and women the victims.

Period of Investigation

The interviewing period extended from April 1976 until September 1976 (hereafter cited as the Research Interval). During this period, the researcher and his associates answered the research telephone in accordance with the published ads. The interviews were not accomplished at a uniform rate throughout the Research Interval since the subjects selected the time and the date for the interview.

Telephone Interviews

Before the first newspaper appearance of the ad, the researcher had a private telephone with an unlisted number installed in his apartment.

During the Research Interval the researcher and his associates answered 182 telephone calls on the research line. The exigencies of life and several inevitable conflicts in schedule created a few periods during the Research Interval when neither the researcher nor his associates were available to answer the phone. Calculation of the number of telephone calls which occurred during these periods was not possible.

Of the 182 telephone calls answered by the researcher and his associates, 50 resulted in interviews included in this investigation. In 106 (58.2%) of the telephone calls there was absolutely no caller response after the phone was answered. In 78 (41.8%) of the telephone calls there was some communication between the interviewer and the respondents. Fifty-five (30%) of the calls led to complete interviews. Of these 55, three interviews were discarded because the respondent indicated that he was not a rapist although he felt he might become one, one interview was discarded because the description of the rape by the Saudi-Arabian respondent did not match the operational definition of rape employed in this investigation; one interview was discarded because the respondent described a homosexual rape.

The Interviewers and Length of the Interview

The telephone interviews ranged from 30 to 50 minutes. The average interview lasted approximately 42 minutes. That the sample size was as large as it was and that the interviews lasted as long as they did is remarkable considering that with one exception the respondents were calling at their own expense.

The interviews were conducted by the principal investigator (a male), or one of two female associates. One of the female interviewers was a Registered Nurse and the other was an Associate Professor at the Claremont Graduate School. Each interviewer had considerable experience in conducting research interviews.

The interviewers attempted to treat the respondents with compassion, to remain nonjudgmental, and to recognize each respondent's need for communication and expression of feeling. Each interviewer probed to obtain amplification with respect to a caller's response while recognizing the respondent's right to decide the degree to which he would respond.

Research Procedure

The research procedure began with the newspaper ad. When the research telephone rang, the interviewer routinely answered "Rape Research Project." If the caller responded, and many did not, the interviewer read the following introductory statement: "This interview is designed to gather information of interest to psychologists about males who have raped women. Obviously, this information is highly personal and I would like to assure you that at no time during the interview will you be asked for your name or address or for any information which may inadvertently reveal the same." If the caller did not hang up after the reading of the introductory statement, the interview was begun.

During the interview the caller was never asked for his name or address or for any information that might lead to the same. At the end of the interview, the interviewer thanked the respondent for his time and cooperation.

The Research Instrument: Nature and Design

The dearth of good theory and definitive data on the rapist made it impractical to develop many specific hypotheses that could be tested. The existence, however, of ample literature on the subject of rape (very little of which is empirical), allowed for the formulation of a series of questions which might provide new and important data on the rapist and his perception of the crime. Using this broad literature as a guide, an interview schedule consisting of 122 questions was developed. The first part of the interview schedule obtained basic demographic data on the respondents (e.g., race, age, marital status, occupation, military service, arrest record, income, educational attainment, family size, drug use patterns, sex history, and the like). The second part concerned the respondent's involvement and experience in the rape of women (e.g., the number of rapes commited, the setting, circumstances surrounding victim selection, use of weapon, amount of force or violence, motivation for the behavior, and the like).

RESULTS

Background Characteristics of the Respondents

In the six months Research Interval, 50 self-selected male rapists completed the interview schedule. Twenty-six percent of the respondents indicated that they had raped only one women prior to the interview, while 74% indicated that they had raped on more than one occasion (Table 1). Forty percent of the subjects had raped more than twice, but less than seven times.

In response to a question concerning the number of women they had raped, several respondents were unable to recall exactly the number and offered only an estimate (e.g., one respondent indicated that he had raped from 10 to 12 women over a period of 6 years). Taking the lowest number offered by these subjects as a conservative estimate, the total sample accounts for the rapes of least 252 women. Twenty (40%) of the respondents reproted having raped on at least one occasion within the year preceding the interview. Another 40% had raped between 1 and 4 years earlier, 18% had not raped for from 5 to 10 years and 2% had not raped for over 10 years (Table 1). Fourteen (28%) of the subjects indicated that they had raped within the 6 months preceding the interview. Data on the dynamics, setting, and circumstances surrounding the rapes described by the respondents has been presented elsewhere. (Smithyman, 1978).

At the time of the interview, the respondents were between 18 and 52 years old. The median age of the group was 27 years. At the time of the sexual assaults described, the subjects were between 14 and 40 years old, with the majority (78%) between 17 and 29. Ethnically, 45 (90%) of the respondents were Caucasian. Twenty-six percent of the respondents were married (including common-law) at the

TABLE 1
Rapes Committed by Respondents and
Time Elapsed Since Last Rape

	N	%
Rapes Committed:		
One	13	26
Two	10	20
Three	9	18
Four–Six	11	22
More Than Seven	7	14
Time Elapsed Since Last Rape:		
Less Than One Year	20	40
One–Four Years	20	40
Five–Ten Years	9	18
Ten Years or More	1	2

time of the interview. Further analysis indicated that 25 (50%) of the subjects had been legally married at some time and that 18 (36%) had been divorced at least once. The data on the educational attainment of the respondents reflected that a high proportion (84%) of the subjects had completed high school. Indeed, 29 (58%) of the respondents had matriculated at a college or university.

At the time of the interview, only 6 (12%) of the respondents were unemployed. Fifty-six percent of the respondents worked in blue collar occupations (laborer, craftsman, operative, foreman); twenty-one (42%) of the respondents were employed in white collar occupations (clerical, sales, teacher, managerial, professional). Thirty-three (66%) of the respondents reported an income of $10,000 per year or more. Eight of the subjects reported an income of $7,999 per year or less, while 8 (16%) of the respondents reported an income of $20,000 per year or more. The median income for the sample was $12,105. Generally, the income reported by the respondents varied in accordance with occupational type.

Given the educational achievement, occupational status, and income of the respondents, it was not surprising to find that 36 (72%) of the respondents had never been arrested.

Further analysis indicated that 11 of the 14 respondents who had been arrested on one or more occasions had never been convicted of a felony. Three (6%) of the respondents had been arrested on a morals or sex charge (including rape) and 2 had been convicted.

Seventeen (34%) of the respondents had been in the military. Two subjects had served as officers and the remaining 15 had served as enlisted men. Eight of the 17 had been in combat, and 16 of the 17 received an honorable discharge.

Forty-two (84%) of the respondents were raised in homes where mother and father figures, as conventionally understood, were present for the greater part of the respondents' youth.

Indeed, 39 (78%) of the respondents reported having growing up in the intact homes of their natural parents who were and remained married to each other. Although surveys such as this make it difficult to obtain definitive information on the qualitative dimensions of important primary relationships, it was interesting to note that 34 (68%) of the respondents felt that their relationships to their parents could best be described as "average" or "above average" and that 32 (64%) of the respondents perceived the relationship between their parents to have ranged from "average" to "very good, warm and affectionate."

For the most part, the respondents appeared to have been raised in families which were not educationally disadvantaged. Only 18% of the mothers and an equal percentage of the fathers had not completed high school. Indeed, 32% of the respondents' fathers and 18% of their mothers were college graduates.

Although presumably most the respondents' lived within the boundaries of metropolitan Los Angeles at the time of the interview, 23 (46%) of the respondents indicated that they had grown up in small towns or rural settings.

Social-Sexual History of the Respondents

Previous studies have not, for the most part, provided students of rape with a great deal of information about the rapist's sexual and social development. From the data gathered in this investigation, several interesting findings on the respondents' socialization have been selected for presentation.

Thirty-eight (76%) of the respondents had engaged in sex play with other children during their prepubertal years.

Thirteen (26%) indicated that this sex play had been limited in both scope and frequency, while 14 (28%) felt that their sex play had been quite extensive. Thirty-three (66%) of the respondents described their experiences as pleasant, and 4 (8%) felt that they had approached these experiences with indifference. Twenty-four of the respondents who had engaged in childhood sex play had experienced no guilt as a result of these experiences, while 14 indicated having experienced some guilt in this regard. Probing by the interviewers indicated that the basis for these guilt feelings was related to the violation of parental prohibitions against such behavior.

Forty-seven (94%) of the respondents had begun masturbating by age 13. Twenty-seven (54%) of the respondents reported never having experienced any anxiety or guilt related to masturbation. Four respondents had experienced considerable guilt over this behavior during periods when masturbating frequency was quite high.

The respondents were asked to indicate when they had first engaged in a particular form of sexual behavior. As indicated, the respondents had engaged in substantial amounts of heterosexual activity at a relatively early age, with progression toward more sophisticated forms of sexual expression as they advanced through high school.

Only 7 (14%) of the subjects experienced their first sexual intercourse after age 18. Thirty-four (68%) of the respondents indicated that their first sexual intercourse had occured with a partner with whom they had no substantial emotional committment, and 41 (82%) of the subjects found the event very pleasurable. Twenty-six (52%) of the respondents indicated that their first sexual intercourse had been planned or at least expected.

When asked to compare the extent of their premarital sexual activity with that of their age mates, 23 (46%) of the respondents felt that they had engaged in more sexual activity and an equal percentage felt that they had engaged in less.

Thirty-two (64%) of the subjects indicated that they had never had a homosexual relationship. Twelve of the 18 respondents who had homosexual experiences indicated that these encounters had basically been early childhood experiences. Only 2 subjects reported frequent homosexual experiences during the period extending from adolescence through the time of the research interview.

Surprisingly, 19 (38%) of the respondents reported some heterosexual contact with a member of their family. Eleven respondents indicated that this incestuous behavior occurred with a sister. Only one respondent indicated that he had sexual intercourse with his natural mother.

Twenty-six (52%) of the respondents reported that during high school they had dated on an average from between once every two weeks to once per week. The remaining 24 subjects were almost equally divided between those who dated more frequently and those who dated less. To examine the subject's perceived social adjustment, they were asked to compare their popularity during high school with that of other members of their social group. Equal percentages felt themselves to have been more and less popular than other members of their immediate social group (42% vs. 36%).

DISCUSSION

Because many rape victims are reluctant to report their rape to the police, and because law enforcement agencies do not solve most crimes or obtain convictions (UCR, 1977), an untold number of rapists, perhaps as many as a half million per year by current estimates, go "undetected." Thus, there is virtually no way to determine currently the "true" parameters of the population of males who rape. Certainly, there is no way of gauging whether subjects in this sample represent the population of males who have raped women. Almost all previous studies of the rapist have studied convicted, imprisoned rapists and are thus biased toward a population known to be deficient with respect to a variety of socioeconomic indicators. The present study altered the traditional focus in studies of the rapist by seeking males within the broader socity (i.e., the noninstitutionalized community) who had raped and who would voluntarily participate in an anonymous telephone interview. This sample, too, is clearly biased; it includes only males who read the advertisement for the research project in a selected paper and who were willing to risk sharing the details of their participation in criminal behavior with an unknown researcher.

Investigations of imprisoned rapists have not discussed the number of rapes committed by their subjects, due in large part, no doubt, to a reluctance of researchers to ask about crimes for which the subjects have not been prosecuted, and to the presumed reluctance of the subjects to disclose their involvement in crimes for which they have not been tried for fear of further legal entanglement. That 74% of the respondents in this study had raped more than once, and that an additional 32% had raped on more than 4 occasions is quite a significant finding, indicating that a high percentage of rapists not caught by law enforcement officials may indeed go on to rape again. Albert De Salvo, for example, the man presumed to be the Boston Strangler, is thought to have committed over 2,000 rapes in addition to 13 rape-murders during his infamous career (Frank, 1966).

Previous investigations have not obtained data on the age that the rapist began his assaultive behavior on women, nor the age at which his behavior terminated. As noted, 70% of the respondents in this study were 24 years of age or younger at the time of their first rape, and 52% were in the same age group at the time of their last rape. Twenty percent of the respondents had participated in rapes after reaching age 25. Only 6 (12%) of the respondents raped after age 34. Although previous studies have not examined their sexual assault careers of their subjects, they have found (e.g., Amir, 1971; Queen's Bench Foundation, 1975; UCR, 1977) the highest proportion of either incarcerated or arrested rapists to have been in the 24 and under age grouping at the time of the detected offense; only a small percentage were over age 34.

The enthic makeup of the sample was comparable with some studies and not with others; some researchers have intentionally examined a particular ethnic group (e.g., Gebhard et al., 1965 included in their study only males who in this society would be considered white) and others have employed whatever subjects were available for investigation in accordance with the sampling plan adopted (e.g., Amir, 1972). The sampling method in this investigation revealed a strong Caucasian bias, due perhaps to the circulation patterns of the newspapers where the ad appeared.

As with the ethnic makeup of the sample, the data on the marital status of the respondents is consistent with some previous studies and inconsistent with others. Amir (1971) found that 83% of the rapists in the Philadelphia police files had never been married, and observed that the majority of previous investigations had found rapists to be among the unmarried. Similarly, the Queen's Bench Foundation (1975) investigation found that 93.2% of the convicted rapists in their study were single at the time of the offense. Gebhard et al. (1965), by contrast, found that 84 (60%) of the imprisoned rapists in their study were married at the time they were interviewed and, presumably, at the time they had committed the sexual assault for which they were imprisoned. As noted, 50% of the subjects in this investigation were legally married prior to the interview.

Studies which find a low proportion of rapists to be married explicitly or implicitly use this finding to support the argument that rapists have been inadequately socialized and are thus not capable of forming intensive relationships with women. That 50% of the respondents in the current investigation were legally married is important for it indicates that not all rapists are deficient in those skills necessary to establish relatively long-lasting and, to some degree, satisfactory heterosexual relationships. Combined with the findings that the respondents had had relatively "normal" dating experiences prior to marriage, and that they felt they had had relatively positive social relationships with peers, the data on the marital status of the respondents provides an interesting counterpoint to the idea that rapists are deficient in those social skills which keep "normal" men from raping women.

One of the most durable issues in the literature on sexual deviance in general, and on the rapist in particular, has been the search for evidence of intellectual impairment. Although never explicitly stated, the logic underlying this search assumes that men who rape women lack the customary standards of judgment and reasoning and must, therefore, be different from ordinary men. Some studies have found that the IQ scores of rapists are lower than one would expect from a "normal" population (e.g., Gillin, 1935; Gebhard et al., 1965; Ruff et al., 1976; Svalastoga, 1962). However, there have been almost an equal number of studies (e.g., Forsch and Bromberg, 1939; Glueck, 1954; and Perdue and Lester, 1972) which have found rapists to have roughly the same intelligence spread as the general population.

Because of the mixed results obtained over a rather long period of time from different prison settings using a variety of measuring instruments, the composite picture of the rapist's intelligence is at best inconclusive. Even if there was agreement among the majority of studies, one would be forced to ask how representative these imprisoned rapists are for generalizing about the entire population of males who rape.

Although no standard scale for measuring intelligence was included in the interview schedule, the findings on the educational attainment of the respondents challenges the assumption that rapists are lacking in the customary standards of reasoning and judgment. Further, the findings are generally inconsistent with previous studies which have reported on the educational attainment of rapists. Gebhard et al. (1965) concluded that most studies of imprisoned sex offenders have generally shown them to have received less education than members of other prison groups. The Queen's Bench Foundation (1975) study of incarcerated California rapists found that 82.2% of the sample had only a high school education or less. The 58% of the respondents in this study who had matriculated at a college or university seems to counter the assumption that "the rapist" is necessarily educationally disadvantaged or suffers from diminished intellectual capacity and attendant social dysfunctioning.

The data on the number of respondents who worked in white collar or professional occupations (42%) also contrast remarkably with both previous findings and popular mythology. Gebhard et al. (1965), for example, found that only 16.4% of their sample of imprisoned rapists could qualify occupationally as Lower White collar; there were not subjects who were classified as either Upper White collar or Professional and Executive. Amir (1971) likewise found that 90% of the rapists in his study belonged to the lower part of the occupational scale (i.e., from semiskilled laborers down). Only one subject in Amir's study qualified for the "professional, technical and kindred" group. The Queen's Bench Foundation (1975) study found only 24.7% of their incarcerated sample to be in the semiprofessional (e.g., clerical, sales, and so forth) category and no subjects who qualified for a higher occupational designation, with the remainder in labor or service occupations. As expected, studies of imprisoned rapists generally find them to cluster among the lower occupational status groups. The data on the occupational background of the respondents in the current study suggest that the rapist can come from virtually any occupational group, and that it is impossible to make a general statement about the association between occupational status and rape.

Data on the criminal background of the respondents which indicate that 72% of the respondents had never been arrested for any offense, and that only 6% had ever been convicted for a felony, contrast markedly with that obtained in previous studies. In Amir's (1971) investigation, for example, 49% of the 1,292 rapists studied had a prior arrest record and 13% of those arrested had been previously charged for a sex crime.

Gebhard et al. (1965) found that 96% of their rapists had been convicted of some crime by age 30, and that two-thirds of the sample had committed at least one prior offense that had cost them a full year or more of prison time. Over half of the prior convictions had been for sex offenses. The Queen's Bench Foundation (1976) findings were similar. Seventy-eight percent of their subjects had been charged with nonsexual offenses and 70% had at least one prior rape charge.

The rapists participating in the current study contrast with many of our expectations. Amir, for example, assumed on the basis of both his findings and his reading of the literature that "Whatever method or material used, rapists emerge as socially unprivileged in their occupation, their education and their social status (1972: 72)." Although the respondents participating in the current research did include males who could certainly be classified as "socially unprivileged," the large proportion of respondents who did not appear to have suffered from extreme social deprivation suggests that theoretical assumptions about rapists and their crimes derived from Amir's data and conceptualization will be overly restrictive.

The demographic indices obtained in this investigation provide a formidable challenge to the generality of Amir's (1971) "sub-culture of violence" theory of rape which locates proviolent sexual norms among individuals and groups in the lower social strata (in what Amir referred to as the lower class Negro-subculture). The demographic backgrounds of the rapists in this study suggest that males at virtually all levels of the social structure can be involved in rape and thus challenges our traditional views of the rapist. The data indicates that males at a variety of social and economic positions may rape, and that aggressive sexual behavior is not exclusively confined to a particular social class or ethnic group. Indeed, the data gathered here provide empirical support for the undocumented feminist contention that our culture socializes males to be potential rapists.

Brownmiller (1975: 176), for example notes that "The typical American rapist is no weirdo, psychoshizophrenic beset by timidity, sexual deprivation, and a domineering wife or mother. Although the psychorapist . . . certainly does exist . . . he is the exception and not the rule. The typical American perpetrator of forcible rape is little more than an aggressive, hostile youth who chooses to do violence to women." Feminists Medea and Thompson (1974: 20-36) echo Brownmiller's sentiments. They assert that "Most men in our country are potential rapists . . . Normal red-blooded American boys are capable of . . . [raping], not in isolation, not in dark and lonely alleys, not in the jungles of Vietnam, but in their own fraternity house with the approval and participation of their peers. The rapist is the man next door."

Previous investigations of rapists have, for the most part, failed to explore aspects of family, social, and sexual development and therefore provide little systematic information to compare the respondents participating in this report. An examination of the data obtained here is remarkable for the absence of indices which readily confirm popular expectations about the inadequate social development of rapists. As a group, the respondents reported having experienced relatively good family adjustment within basically "intact" homes, and described relatively positive social relationships with peers during adolescence.

Several major implications emerge from the findings in this investigation. The first has to do with the characteristic image of the rapist which is shaped by our knowledge of his coercive sexual behavior. Knowing that a male has raped tends to overshadow interest in virtually every other aspect of his behavior, dramatizing both the importance of the event in his life and, perhaps, obscuring aspects of his everyday social functioning which he shares with virtually every other member of the society. This overemphasis on his sexually agressive behavior tends to blind us to the fact that the rapist is more like than unlike the majority of males in our society. While a study of males who rape must examine those aspects of their behavior which relate to sexual assault, it is perhaps an oversimplification to assume that the entire life of the rapist is consumed solely by constant and uncontrollable sexual desire. Only the smallest time segments appear to be spent in such activities, with the remaining majority of time spent in acceptable activities (e.g., work, school, marriage, and so forth).

While many important aspects of the lives of the men participating in this study must remain unknown, the data presented in this section did highlight some of the more salient aspects of their overall life experiences. Along almost every dimension examined, these men did not differ markedly from the majority of males in our culture. Indeed, there appears to be such a wide variety of backgrounds among males who rape that no sweeping generalizations about them should be made. Except for their admission of rape, these respondents seemed indistinguishable from most other males in our society, accounting to some degree perhaps for their remaining "undetected."

The second major implication of these findings had to do with the fact that having raped is not indicative of an attribute (i.e., something which one either is or is not, such as male or female, or something which one has or has not, such as blue or brown eyes). This is perhaps obvious but too often ignored. That being a rapist is not an attribute means that some of our traditional ways of viewing both rape and the rapist must be modified. That is, the traditional tendency has located the sole source of the difficulty within the male who rapes, tending to see him as emotionally disturbed. As additional data gathered by the author makes clear (Smithyman, 1978), this view ignores the social and cultural contexts from which the behavior of the rapist emerges. It seems likely from both previous research evidence (e.g., Amir, 1971) as well as from the general characters of the data gathered here, that many rapists tend to be more "normal" than "abnormal" when measured by mental pathology. Thus, research designed to establish that rapists are like "this" while nonrapists are like "that" would appear to have little to contribute to our understanding of both the man and his crime.

The data gathered and presented here on the background of the respondents, combined with the author's additional findings (Smithyman, 1978) which examined the variety of social circumstances and varying social dynamics that can result in an act of rape (i.e., forced penetration of the vagina) may not always reflect pathological deviation in the male. The occurrence of a rape may, in many instances, be the logical outcome of a prevailing set of social and cultural norms, which set up males to become rapists and women to become rape victims.

REFERENCES

AMIR, M. (1971) Patterns in Forcible Rape. Chicago: Univ. of Chicago Press.

ANASTASI, A. (1968) Psychological Testing. New York: Macmillan.

BROWNMILLER, S. (1975) Against Our Will: Men, Women and Rape. New York: Simon & Schuster.

BURGESS, A. W., and L. L. HOLMSTROM (1974) Rape: Victims of Crises. Bowie, MD: Robert J. Brady.

COHEN, M. L., M. A. GAROFALO, and T. SEGHORN (1971) "The psychology of rapists." Seminars in Psychiatry 3: 307-327.

CONNELL, N. and C. WILSON [eds.] (1974) Rape: The First Sourcebook for Women. New York: New American Library.

FRANK, G. (1966) The Boston Strangler. New York: New American Library.

Federal Bureau of Investigation (1977) Department of Justice Uniform Crime Reports-1976. Washington, DC: Government Printing Office.

FROSCH, J. and W. BROMBERG (1939) "The sex offender: a psychiatric study." Amer. J. of Orthopsychiatry 9: 761-776.

GEBHARD, P. H., J. H. GAGNON, W. B. POMEROY, and C. V. CHRISTENSON (1975) Sex Offenders: An Analysis of Types. New York: Harper & Row.

GILLIN, J. L. (1953) "Social background of sex offenders and murderers." Social Forces 14: 232-239.

GLUECK, B. C. (1954) "Psychodynamic patterns in the sex offender." Psychiatric Q. 29: 1-21.

GOLDNER, N. S. (1972) "Rape as a heinous but understudied offense." J. of Criminal Law, Criminology and Police Sci. 63: 402-407.

GRIFFIN, S. (1971) "Rape: the all-American crime." Ramparts: 26-35.

GUTTMACHER, M. S. and H. WEIHOFEN (1952) Psychiatry and the Law. New York: Norton.

HOROS, C. V. (1974) Rape: The Private Crime, A Social Horror. New Canaan, OH: Tobey Publishing.

KARPMAN, B. (1954) The Sexual Offender and His Offenses. New York: The Julian Press.

MEDEA, A. and K. THOMPSON (1974) Against Rape: A Survival Manual For Women. New York: Farrar, Straus & Giroux.

National Commission on the Causes and Prevention of Violence (1969) Crimes of

Violence: A Staff Report. D. J. Mulvihill and M. M. Tumin (eds.) Washington, DC: Government Printing Office.

PERDUE, W. C. and D. LESTER (1972) "Personality characteristics of rapists." Perceptual and Motor Skills 35: 514.

Queen's Bench Foundation (1975) Rape: Prevention and Resistance. San Francisco: Author.

ROSE, V. L. (1976) "Rape as a social problem: a feminist and social movement perspective." Presented at the annual meeting of the Pacific Sociological Association, San Diego, California.

RUFF, C. F., D. I. TEMPLAR, and J. L. AYERS (1976) "The intelligence of rapists." Archives of Sexual Behavior 5: 327-371.

RUSSELL, D.E.H. (1975) The Politics of Rape: The Victim's Perspective. New York: Stein & Day.

SMITHYMAN, S. D. (1978) "The undetected rapist." Ph.D. dissertation, Claremont Graduate School.

SVALASTOGA, K. (1962) "Rape and social structure." Pacific Soc. Rev. 5: 48-53.

John R. Hepburn

Pennsylvania State University

Daniel J. Monti

University of Missouri, St. Louis

8

VICTIMIZATION, FEAR OF CRIME, AND ADAPTIVE RESPONSES AMONG HIGH SCHOOL STUDENTS

National concern has turned most recently to victimization and fear of crime among youth in a specific and universal social setting—the schools. A national opinion poll (Gallup, 1977) of 1000 teenagers reported, for example, that nearly 1 in 5 fear for their personal safety while at school, that nearly one-fourth had property stolen at school, and that over 10% had property destroyed or damaged. An extensive analysis of school-related victimization has been undertaken by the National Institute of Education (1977), using a mail survey of over 4,000 schools, on-site interviews at 642 schools, and case studies of 10 schools. The findings indicate the scope of school-related victimization: 40% of the robberies and 35% of the personal attacks against student-aged teenagers occur in school; between 74 and 98% of all offenses except trespassing and breaking and entering are committed by students enrolled in the school; the annual cost of school crimes is estimated at $200 million.

The N.I.E. study also indicates that a substantial proportion of students alter their behavior due to recent victimization or fear of victimization. Eight percent of the large city junior high students stayed at home at least one day in a month due to fear of victimization, a third reported that they avoided three or more places within the school due to fear of victimization, and more than a quarter of those victimized by attack or robbery reportedly brought "something to school for protection" on some occasions. Precautionary activities as adaptive responses to a fear of victimization have received little attention to date, yet it is apparent that the fear of crime alienates and isolates its victims (McIntyre, 1967; Brooks, 1974; Conlin, 1975).

The value of the N.I.E. victimization study lies in its concern with the school. Other research efforts have examined victimization among youth, but they have neglected the school as a social setting. Feyerherm and Hindelang (1974), for example, selected a sample of white high school students from a medium-sized city, but did not examine the school setting *per se*. Their results indicate that males are only slightly more likely than females to report having been victimized, but that females are substantially more likely than males to indicate that they are fearful when walking on neighborhood streets after dark. Fear of crime was found to be unrelated to victimization and victims reported the incident to the police with the same frequency regardless of offense type or sex of victim. Savitz et al. (1977) report the results of interviews with black and white juveniles attending various schools in Philadelphia. Among the findings are the absence of a relationship between victimization and adaptive responses. It is evident, however, that blacks are more likely than whites to engage in the adaptive responses of avoidance and carrying a weapon.

In summary, the victimization analyses conducted by Feyerherm and Hindelang and by Savitz et al. are valuable additions to the literature because (1) they concern teenagers, a population neglected by most studies; and (2) they examine direct victimization, fear of victimization, and adaptive response patterns. The value of the N.I.E. report rests largely in its examination of the schools. To be sure, the report reveals a number of interesting findings, but it raises more questions than it answers due to its methodological weaknesses (Emrich, 1978; Rubel, 1978) and failure to incorporate desirable multivariate analyses. Our research which uses a multivariate analysis, examines school-related victimization, fear of victimization, and adaptive responses among students.

RESEARCH METHODS

Useable data were available on 1799 students, representing nearly the entire population of a high school in the city of St. Louis. Each respondent anonymously completed a short, self-administered questionnaire which was both physically distributed and verbally presented to reduce errors attributable to reading and comprehension difficulties. Since the data were obtained while students were assembled in their first-period classes, the data represent all students in attendance at that time. The respondents range in age from 13 to 20, with a mean age of 16.1 years. Males comprise 47.8% of the respondents; 75.8% of the responding students are white.

Fear of crime is operationalized by the student's response to an item asking whether he or she has "been afraid that someone will hurt or bother you at school." Victimization was measured by responses to four items, each of which sought the presence or absence of victimization "during the present school year." Since the data were obtained in April, victimization refered to an eight-month period rather than a calendar year. Three forms of adaptive response were used in the analysis. Each respondent was asked whether he or she had avoided certain places with the school, had avoided certain groups of students, or had "brought something" to school for protection because "someone might hurt or bother you."

Finally, each student was asked to indicate his or her level of approval or disapproval for 10 kinds of behavior if engaged in by a friend.[1] Although a single dimension was sought, factor analysis revealed that the four minor kinds of behavior loaded on one factor and the six more serious sorts of behavior loaded on a separate factor. Since our interest is in adaptive responses to relatively serious behavior, the minor behavior tolerance scores are omitted from consideration, and the summated score of the remaining six items, scored such that the higher value reflects a higher degree of tolerance, represent tolerance of serious behavior.[2]

The victimization items, and the respective percentage indicating they had been victimized at least once, are: (1) "Did anyone take money or things directly from you by force, weapons or threats?" [4.3%]; (2) "Did anyone steal something from your desk, locker or other place at school?" [39.9%]; (3) "Did anyone physically attack and hurt you?" [7.2%]; (4) "Have you been in a fight?" [20.6%]. Although the items are not identical to those in other studies of victimization among teenagers, a comparison indicates that the level of victimization among these respondents is similar to that noted elsewhere. Feyerherm and Hindelang report that 7% of the males and 2% of the females were physically assaulted in one year. Gallup's survey reveals that 4% of the respondents were physically assaulted in one year, and the National Institute of Education reports that 6.2% of the males and 2.4% of the females were attacked during one month. The St. Louis school survey indicates that 7.2% were assault during the school year.

Similarly, the 4.3% of this group who indicated that something was taken by force compared favorably to the 3% of the males and 2% of the females who reported such an occurrence in the survey by Feyerherm and Hindelang, and the 6.3% of the males and 2.7% of the females reported by the National Institute of Education. Furthermore, whereas Feyerherm and Hindelang report only 14% had property stolen, Gallup reports 36.0%, and this survey finds 39.9% who report being so victimized. These findings suggest that the level of victimization reported by the respondents is not atypical.[3]

FINDINGS

Initial analyses of victimization, fear of crime, and adaptive responses by age, race, and sex are presented in Table 1. Victimization had been recoded to indicate the presence or absence of any of the four specific victimization items reported above, and nearly half the respondents indicated at least one form of victimization during the school year. Victimization was found to be significantly more prevalent among older than younger respondents and among males than females.[4] Contrary to the National Institute of Education Report, the minority group was no more likely to be victimized than the majority group. This finding is affirmed when age and sex are controlled simultaneously.

The data in Table 1 also indicate that younger and white respondents were significantly more likely to report fear of crime than older and nonwhite respondents. Simultaneous controls by age and sex, however, revealed that the difference between whites and nonwhites was sustained only among the older respondents. Nonetheless, a higher percentage of younger respondents than older respondents reported a fear of crime when both race and sex were controlled.

The only significant difference in avoidance of places was by sex: More females indicated an avoidance of places than did males. Yet simultaneous controls for age and race indicated that females were no more likely than males to indicate an avoidance of places. It appears, rather, that older white females report avoidance of place more than do older nonwhite females and, although not statistically significant, more younger respondents report avoidance of places than do their older race-sex counterparts, with the exception of white females.

An analysis of avoidance of groups revealed a similar result. Whites were significantly more likely than nonwhites to report avoidance of groups, yet this racial difference was minimized when controlling for age and sex. Avoidance of gorups was more likely among younger males than younger females, regardless of race, but among older whites than among older nonwhites regardless of sex. That is, avoidance of groups is an adaptive response used by younger males of both racial groups; among older students, avoidance of groups is an adaptive response more often employed by whites than nonwhites.

Finally, the possession of a weapon was more likely to be an adaptive response of nonwhites than whites and of males than females. Whereas older nonwhites were more likely to carry a weapon than younger nonwhites, it is apparent that possession of a weapon did not differ by age among whites.

These data provide tentative conclusions. Race is unrelated to victimization but significantly associated with both fear of crime and adaptive responses. Whites are more likely than nonwhites to use an avoidance response, and nonwhites are more likely than whites to prepare for an aggressive episode. Age covaries with both fear of crime and victimization (although younger students have greater fear of crime, older students are more victimized) but is unrelated to adaptive responses. Sex is related to victimization and some of the adaptive responses but not to fear of crime. These findings failed to reveal any consistent pattern other than that whites are more likely to avoid groups, and nonwhites are more likely to bring a weapon.

Relevant bivariate correlation coefficients are presented in Table 2. Race and sex are dichotomous variables assuming the value of 0 (white; female) or 1 (nonwhite; male). An interval level of measurement is also used for age. Victimization has been scored to indicate the number of victimization items to which the respondent indicated at least one occurrence; therefore, victimization ranges from 0, or no victimization reported, to 4, victimization at least once on each of the four items. When operationalized in this manner, victimization is more an indication of the scope of the respondent's prior victimization than it is a measure of the frequency of victimization. Fear of crime is dichotomous, with a value of 0 assigned to those who indicate no fear, and a value of 1 assigned to those who indicate having some fear. For each of the three indices of adaptive response—avoid places, avoid groups, bring weapon—are also dichotomous variables, with a 0 assigned to those who never responded in this way, and a 1 assigned to those who indicate they have adapted in such a manner on at least one occasion.

TABLE 1
Victimization, Fear of Crime and Adaptive Responses by Age, Race and Sex of Respondents

	Victimization % Report One or More Times	Fear of Crime % Report Being Afraid	Adaptive Response % Agree, Avoid Place	% Agree, Avoid Groups	% Agree, Bring Weapon
TOTAL	49.4	40.0	13.5	23.7	15.7
N* =	(1775)	(1777)	(1782)	(1783)	(1776)
Age:					
15 or younger (N=595)	41.4[a]	46.7[a]	14.6	25.4	14.9
16 or older (N=1160)	52.9	36.6	13.1	22.9	15.8
Race:					
White (N=1346)	48.4	43.9[a]	14.3	25.5[b]	13.5[a]
Nonwhite (N=430)	51.6	27.4	10.9	17.8	22.4
Sex:					
Male (N=847)	55.6[a]	38.3	11.6[b]	23.0	23.2[a]
Female (N=924)	43.2	41.3	15.2	24.3	8.7
Age X Race X Sex:					
15 or younger					
White male (N=192)	47.4	50.8	13.6	29.4	22.8
Nonwhite male (N=57)	51.8	40.4	17.5	26.3	19.6
White female (N=262)	33.9	47.6	13.5	24.2	7.1
Nonwhite female (N=82)	39.0	35.8	15.9	16.3	14.6
16 or older					
White male (N=433)	57.6	36.2[b]	11.3	21.7	20.7[b]
Nonwhite male (N=143)	59.9	26.1	7.0	16.8	29.4
White female (N=450)	46.6	45.6[a]	18.1[b]	28.6[b]	5.0[a]
Nonwhite female (N=134)	49.6	19.4	9.0	14.9	19.4

*N = The number who responded to the item(s).   a = p $<$ .001.   b = p $<$ .05.

TABLE 2
Bivariate Correlation Coefficients, Standardized Regression
Coefficients and Joint Linear Effects of Independent
Variables on Each Adaptive Response

	Avoid Groups		Avoid Places		Carry Weapon	
	r	b	r	b	r	b
Age	.03	−.009	−.02	−.004	.02	−.013
Race	−.09	−.019	−.04	.011	.11	.106
Sex	−.02	.000	−.05	−.045	.20	.141
Victimization	.03	.106	.16	.142	.27	.224
Fear of Crime	.40	.370	.36	.339	.08	.084
Tolerance of Serious Behaviors	−.14	−.113	−.12	−.095	.20	.143
R^2		.18		.16		.14

The correlation coefficients were attenuated due to the restricted variation occurring with some of the variables.[5] Nonetheless, an examination of the coefficients reported in Table 2 suggests that victimization is meaningfully associated with avoidance of places and carrying a weapon. Fear of crime was found to be strongly related to avoidance of both places and groups, but not with carrying a weapon. Indeed, the adaptive responses of avoidance of places and avoidance of groups covary (r = .48), but neither demonstrated a substantial association with bringing a weapon (r = .08, .06). Tolerance of serious behavior was negatively related to both avoidance responses and positively related to carrying a weapon. Finally, it is noteworthy that victimization was weakly associated with fear of crime (r = .12) and tolerance of serious behavior (r = .14) and that the relation between fear of crime and tolerance was low (r = .10).

These findings suggest that adaptive responses cannot be uniformly attributed to victimization, fear of crime, or tolerance of behavior. Specifically, the zero-order correlation coefficients suggest linkages requiring additional analysis which will indicate the relative explanatory importance of each variable when controlling for the effects of other variables. This information is provided in Table 2, which presents the results of a stepwise regression of each of the adaptive responses on the other variables.

Fear of crime was the major explanatory variable in the simultaneous regression of avoidance of groups on all independent variables. In fact, not one of the other independent variables significantly added to the predictive accuracy once fear of crime was entered into the equation. Similarly, fear of crime was the only factor to significantly predict avoidances of places. Although the six independent variables explained 18% of the variation in avoidance of groups and 16% of the variation in avoidance of places, fear of crime accounted for 16% and 13% of the explained variation. In contrast, victimization accounted for a significant amount of the variation in the adaptive response of carrying a weapon. Of the remaining independent variables, only tolerance of serious behaviors added significantly to the amount of variation explained after victimization was entered into the equation. These findings indicate that adaptive responses of avoidance of places and avoidance of groups are accounted for by fear of crime, but carrying a weapon is accounted for by victimization.

CONCLUSION

Although victimization surveys have been used extensively to ascertain more information about the characteristics of offenses, victims, and offenders, few efforts have been directed to examining the relation of victimization to variables of sociological relevance. Furthermore, most of our current information is limited to bivariate relationships among adult samples. Even fewer analyses of victimization among juveniles exist, despite the recent national concern with school related victimization. For these reasons, data obtained from 1,799 students in one senior high school were presented to examine the relation among school-related victimization, fear of crime, and adaptive responses.

Victimization among high school students was found to be weakly associated with age and sex. Race was not associated with victimization, but there was a weak bivariate relation with fear of crime. Avoidance of places was more frequent among females than males, avoidance of groups was more likely among whites than nonwhites, and carrying a weapon was more frequently reported by males and nonwhites than by females and whites. Thus, it appears that victimization is somewhat more extensive among older than younger students and among males than females. Despite their greater victimization, however, older and male students are no more likely to fear crime or avoid places and groups than are younger and female students. Males are more likely to carry a weapon for protection than are females, however. Finally, white students are somewhat more likely than nonwhite students to fear crime, and apparently adapt differently; whites show a slightly greater tendency to avoid groups, blacks show a slightly greater tendency to carry a weapon.

An examination of the independent effects of age, race, sex, victimization, fear of crime, and tolerance of delinquent behavior on indices of adaptive response indicates the relative importance of each variable. Avoidance of groups and avoidance of places are accounted for by fear of crime, but carrying a weapon is largely explained by victimization. Thus it appears that those victimized at school have little fear of crime, and take few steps to avoid it in the future. But, these persons are more likely to carry a weapon should such a situation arise.

Although the relation of victimization and fear of crime to adaptive responses has been examined, this analysis did not attempt to treat the factors that may lead to victimization in schools. One area in need of systematic analysis is the relation of structural variables to victimization and fear of crime. The size of the school, for example, already has received some attention (Berger, 1974; McPartland and McDill, 1977; National Institute of Education, 1977) as a significant factor in explaining school violence and disruption. In addition, there has been mention of the criminogenic influence of class size (Marvin et al., 1977), student-teacher interaction, percentage male and mean student grade point average (National Institute of Education, 1977). Additional structural variables worthy of examination would include racial and socioeconomic composition of student population, racial composition of staff, mean student score on standardized natural tests, and differences in curricula (e.g., tracking). Comparative and longitudinal structural data will enable an examination of the impact of the rapidity and extent of structural change upon victimization and fear of crime.

NOTES

1. A Likert-type response format, ranging from strongly disapprove (value of 1) to strongly approve (value of 5) was used. The 10 items and their mean values are: cheat on test, 2.64; drink beer, wine, or alcohol, 3.54; skip school, 3.16; hurt someone in a fight for the fun of it, 1.56; break school windows, 1.83; smoke marijuana; 3.12; be suspended from school, 2.11; take things of less than $2.00 in value, 1.96; mark up school walls, 2.06; hurt someone in a fight in order to take something from them, 1.51.

2. The 4 minor behavior items are: (1) cheat on a test; (2) drink beer, wine or alcohol; (3) skip school; and (4) smoke marijuana. The remaining 6 items form the measure of tolerance of serious behavior, which has a mean value of 11.04. The item-to-item correlation coefficients range from .22 to .50 and the item-to-total score coefficients range from .62 to .73.

3. These preliminary findings may be typical for similar populations, but it should be noted that they vary considerably from those reported by Savitz et al., who indicated that 30-38% of the black juveniles were robbed and 16-18% were assaulted during a year. Victimization among lower socioeconomic status students in inner-city schools is yet to be fully explored.

4. Because the data can be considered as a population rather than a sample, tests of significance are not required and any observed difference is significant but not necessarily meaningful. By treating the data as a sample and using tests of significance, however, we have established an objective criterion for ascertaining those differences which are of substantive importance. Consequenly, tests of significance are used to test the assumption that the observed difference is different from zero at known levels of probability.

5. The attenuation of correlation and regression coefficients provides for a more conservative estimate of the relationships. This is especially the case with avoidance of place and carrying a weapon, since the amount of variation is dangerously small. This problem is overcome to some degree, however, by the large number of cases which result in less error variance. Nonetheless, error variance due to measurement error is unknown and likely to be underestimated.

REFERENCES

BERGER, M. (1974) Violence in the Schools: Causes and Remedies. Bloomington, IN: Phi Delta Kappa Educational Foundation.

BROOKS, J. (1974) "The fear of crime in the United States." Crime and Delinquency 20 (July): 241-244.

CONKLIN, J. (1975) The Impact of Crime. New York: Macmillan.

EMRICH, R. (1978) "The safe school study report to the Congress: evaluation and recommendations." Crime and Delinquency 24 (July): 266-276.

FEYERHERM, W., and M. HINDELANG (1974) "On the victimization of juveniles: some preliminary results." J. of Research in Crime and Delinquency 11 (January): 40-50.

GALLUP, G. (1977) "Teenagers fear school violence." St. Louis Post-Dispatch (December 21): 5F.

MARVIN, M., R. McCANN, J. CONNOLLY, S. TEMKIN, and P. HENNING (1977) "Current activities in schools," pp. 53-70 in J. McPartland and E. McDill (eds.) Violence In Schools. Lexington, MA: D. C. Heath.

McPARTLAND, J., and E. McDILL (1977) "Research on crime in schools," pp. 3-33 in J. McPartland and E. McDill (eds.) Violence In Schools. Lexington, MA: D. C. Heath.

McINTYRE, J. (1967) "Public attitudes toward crime and law enforcement." Annals 374 (November): 34-46.

National Institute of Education (1977) Violent Schools—Safe Schools: The Safe School Study Report to the Congress. Washington, DC: U.S. Department of Health, Education, and Welfare.

RUBEL, R. (1978) "Analysis and critique of HEW's safe school study report to the Congress." Crime and Delinquency 24 (July): 257-265.

SAVITZ, L., M. LALLI, and L. ROSEN (1977) City Life and Delinquency—Victimization, Fear of Crime and Gang Membership. National Institute for Juvenile Justice and Delinquency Prevention, Law Enforcement Assistance Administration. U.S. Department of Justice. Washington, DC: Government Printing Office.

Mark Blumberg
SUNY, Albany

9

INJURY TO VICTIMS OF PERSONAL CRIMES:
Nature and Extent

INTRODUCTION

This essay used data from the National Crime Survey (NCS) to measure the nature and extent of injury to victims of personal crimes. The analysis contains two sections. In the first, a low threshold definition of injury was used. Thus, victims were separated into two categories: those who received injury and those who did not. This categorization combined victims who received minor injuries (e.g., scratches or bruises) with those who received major injuries (e.g., broken bones). The second section of the study used a higher threshold definition. Victims who received injuries that required medical attention were compared with all other victims.

In addition to examining the nature and extent of injury, analysis was also undertaken to determine the correlates of personal injury. Using both definitions of injury, identical variables in each section were examined to identify their relationship to victim-injury, if any. These variables relate to three general areas: victim characteristics, offender char-

AUTHOR'S NOTE: *Portions of this paper are drawn from research supported by Grant 75-SS-99-6029 awarded to the Criminal Justice Research Center, Albany, New York, by the Statistics Division, National Criminal Justice Information and Statistics Service, Law Enforcement Assistance Administration, U.S. Department of Justice. Points of view or opinions are those of the author and do not necessarily represent the official position of the U.S. Department of Justice.*

acteristics, and situational characteristics. It should be interesting to observe whether the same correlates of personal injury were obtained with both definitions of injury.

This study sought to answer many interesting questions about injury to victims of personal crimes. For example, do demographic characteristics of victims bear any relationship to the risk of injury? What about the demographic characteristics of offenders? Is the risk of injury greater for victims who employ self-protective measures? What relation exists between the presence of an offender with a weapon and personal injury? These and other issues were addressed. However, before the substantive findings of this inquiry are presented, a brief discussion of the methodology and history of the National Crime Survey will be undertaken.

THE NATIONAL CRIME SURVEY

Since 1972, the Bureau of the Census, in conjunction with the Law Enforcement Assistance Administration (LEAA), has been engaged in the systematic collection of information pertaining to criminal victimizations in the United States. The results of their efforts, the National Crime Survey (NCS), consist of interviews with approximately 132,000 individuals in 60,000 households that are interviewed annually to obtain a national stratified probability sample. In this study, data for the years 1974 and 1975 have been combined to insure enough cases for a detailed and reliable statistical analysis.

The National Crime Survey (NCS) collects information pertaining to characteristics of the respondent and of the household, inquiries whether either was the target of a criminal victimization in the previous 6 months, and gathers data relating to the circumstances and consequences of any victimizations reported to the interviewer. From this information, a picture of the extent and character of personal injury victimizations can be drawn.

It should be noted that the NCS elicits information about the personal crimes of assault, rape, larceny,[1] and robbery. Data pertaining to certain household crimes (i.e., burglary, auto theft, and household larceny) are also collected. However, the latter are by definition incidents that do not involve personal injury and, therefore, are excluded from the analysis. Readers wishing a detailed discussion of the issues involved in the design, methodology, and administration of the National Crime Survey are advised to consult Garofalo and Hindelang (1978).

Finally, the reader should be advised that personal crimes in this report are categorized without regard to their corresponding legal criteria. Instead, victimizations were categorized according to the motive of the offender. Offenders in personal crimes may be motivated either by a desire to steal property from the victim or by a desire to harm the victim. Thus victimizations are categorized either as theft-related or nontheft-related. It is believed that this approach is more useful for an analysis of personal injury than combining all personal victimizations or using the legal offense criterion. The former may mask important differences in the data that arise because some offenders seek to steal property and other offenders seek to do bodily harm. The latter approach neglects the fact that offenses may fall within different legal categories but share important characteristics, nonetheless.

THE EXTENT OF PERSONAL INJURY

It is observed from Table 1 that approximately one-quarter (27%) of the victims of personal crimes receive some form of injury. Separate analysis of theft- and nontheft-related incidents indicates that a somewhat greater proportion of the latter result in injury to the victim. This is not surprising given that the intent of offenders in nontheft-related incidents is to do bodily harm to the victim. Despite this fact and despite the low threshold definition of personal injury that is currently being employed, only 3 out of 10 nontheft victims received injury. Clearly, the majority of personal crimes do not result in any injury to the victim regardless of which category (i.e., theft or nontheft) is examined.

TABLE 1

Percentage of Victimizations Resulting in Injury to the Victim
by Type of Victimization and by Selected Victim Characteristics;
United States, 1974-1975

| Victim Characteristics | Type of Victimization | | Total |
	Theft-related	Nontheft-related	
Race of victim			
White	22%[a]	29%	27%
	(2,565,695)[b]	(7,414,628)	(9,980,323)
Black/other	24%	32%	29%
	(812,960)	(1,078,778)	(1,891,738)
Sex of victim			
Male	25%	28%	27%
	(2,041,660)	(5,390,870)	(7,432,530)
Female	20%	31%	28%
	(1,336,996)	(3,102,536)	(4,439,532)
Age of victim			
12-19	22%	34%	31%
	(969,168)	(3,098,560)	(4,067,728)
20-34	23%	27%	26%
	(1,105,130)	(3,652,287)	(4,757,417)
35-49	24%	26%	25%
	(526,613)	(1,048,041)	(1,574,654)
50-64	22%	24%	23%
	(462,492)	(515,786)	(978,278)
65 or older	21%	25%	22%
	(315,252)	(178,732)	(493,984)
Total	23%	29%	27%
	(3,378,655)	(8,493,406)	(11,872,061)

a. Percent of victimizations in cell that resulted in injury to the victim.
b. Estimated number of personal victimizations in cell; base on which percent is computed.

THE EXTENT OF PERSONAL INJURY
AND VICTIM CHARACTERISTICS

At this point, the question of whether the demographic characteristics of victims bear any relation to personal injury shall be addressed. The data in Table 1 indicate that no relations are observed either between the race or sex of victim and personal injury. In general, the proportion of incidents that result in injury is similar for males, females, whites, and black/others.[2]

Turning to the relation between personal injury and age of victim, it is apparent that the data are not as straightforward. Although there is no relation between age of victim and injury for theft-related incidents, the data indicate that some relation exists between age and injury for nontheft-related incidents (see Table 1). Nontheft victimizations directed against individuals in the youngest age category (12-19) are somewhat more likely to result in injury than those directed against the other age categories.

It is interesting to note that the data refute a common misconception about the relation between age of victim and personal injury. It is commonly believed that the elderly have the greatest risk of incurring injury in a criminal victimization. Clearly, the data do not support this notion. It should be noted that this finding is in agreement with that of a victimization survey which employed data from 26 cities (Hochstedler, forthcoming).

Thus, it must be concluded that except for the higher proportion of injuries among young nontheft victims, demographic characteristics of victims do not bear any relation to injury. Having examined this question, attention shall now be turned to the relation between the demographic characteristics of offenders and personal injury to victims.

THE EXTENT OF PERSONAL INJURY AND OFFENDER CHARACTERISTICS

Although the data are not shown in tabular form, the analysis indicates that race of offender bears no relation to injury. Victimizations perpetrated by white offenders are as likely to result in injury to the victim as those perpetrated by black/other offenders. This is true whether theft- or nontheft-related incidents are examined.

The analysis also indicates that sex of offender bears no relation to injury for nontheft-related incidents. However, males are somewhat more likely to inflict injury in theft-related incidents. Twenty-six percent of the theft-related victimizations perpetrated by males resulted in injury compared to 19% of the thefts perpetrated by females. This difference is probably explained by a greater likelihood of male theft offenders pursuing their objectives in incidents where their demands for money or property have been refused. This finding should cause little surprise given the greater physical ability of males to impose their will through force.

Turning to the relationship between personal injury and age of offender, it is apparent that the relations for theft- and nontheft-related incidents point in opposite directions.[3] Theft victimizations committed by young offenders (less than 18 years of age) are somewhat less likely to result in injury to the victim than those committed by older offenders. On the other hand, nontheft victimizations committed by very young offenders (less than 15 years of age) are somewhat more likely to result in injury to the victim. Why this is so is not immediately apparent. However, it is clear that separate analysis of the theft- and nontheft-related victimizations reveals relations that otherwise would be obscured.

Having examined the relations between offender characteristics and injury, the next section will examine the question of how situational characteristics influence the risk of injury.

THE EXTENT OF PERSONAL INJURY AND SITUATIONAL CHARACTERISTICS

The first situational characteristic to be analyzed in terms of its relation to personal injury is the number of offenders involved in the incident. This is followed by an analysis of the relation of injury to the following situational characteristics: whether the victim employed self-protective measures; whether the offender possessed a weapon; and the type of weapon possessed by the offender.

From Table 2, it is apparent that the number of offenders bears no relation to injury for nontheft-related victimizations, but that some relation exists between the variables for theft-related victimizations. Approximately 30% of the nontheft victims received injury regardless of whether one

TABLE 2

Percentage of Victimizations Resulting in Injury to the Victim
by Type of Victimization and by Selected Situational Characteristics;
United States, 1974-1975

Situational Characteristics	Type of Victimization		Total
	Theft-related	Nontheft-related	
Number of offenders[a]			
One	21%[d]	29%	28%
	(1,377,669)[e]	(5,693,042)	(7,070,711)
More than one	30%	30%	30%
	(1,517,501)	(2,579,424)	(4,096,925)
Self-protective measures by victim			
Yes	31%	29%	29%
	(1,439,827)	(5,868,156)	(7,307,983)
No	17%	30%	24%
	(1,938,828)	(2,625,250)	(4,564,078)
Possession of weapon by offender[b]			
Yes	32%	30%	30%
	(1,213,479)	(3,156,783)	(4,370,262)
No	20%	31%	28%
	(1,434,266)	(4,729,125)	(6,163,391)
Type of weapon possessed by offender[c]			
Gun	19%	13%	15%
	(501,069)	(1,138,430)	(1,639,499)
Knife	29%	30%	29%
	(431,465)	(828,765)	(1,260,229)
Other	54%	46%	47%
	(277,982)	(1,199,944)	(1,477,836)

a. Excludes 704,426 victimizations for which the number of offenders was unknown by the victim.
b. Excludes 1,338,407 victimizations in which the victim did not know if the offender possessed a weapon.
c. The number of cases in the column may slightly exceed the number of victimizations in which respondents said that the offender used a weapon because more than one type of weapon was used in some of the victimizations that involved more than one offender.
d. Percent of victimizations in cell that resulted in injury to the victim.
e. Estimated number of personal victimizations in cell; base on which percent is computed.

offender or more than one offender was involved in the incident. On the other hand, 21% of the theft victims who encountered a single offender were injured compared with 30% of such victims who encountered more than one offender (see Table 2). Thus it appears that the risk of injury is somewhat less for theft victims who encounter only one offender than for other victims of personal crimes.

Attention can now be turned to the important question of the relation between personal injury and the employment of self-protective measures by victims. Although no relation is observed between injury and self-protective measures among nontheft victims, theft victims who employed such measures were more likely to be injured than those who did not. Approximately 30% of the nontheft victims were injured regardless of victim response. On the other hand, 31% of the theft victims who employed self-protective measures were injured compared with only 17% of those who did not (see Table 2).[4]

It is important to note that a cause and effect relation between injury and self-protective measures cannot be inferred. Although it is true that theft victims who employed such measures were more likely to be injured, it is not clear whether the self-protective measures preceded or followed the offender's attack. Conceivably, victims may be taking self-protective measures to protect themselves from an attack and not to resist the theft. If this is true, the larger proportion of injuries in this category may be a result of the offender's action and not the response of the victim. Further research on the dynamics of the theft incident will be required to fully answer this question. One possibility that may be uncovered by such research is that a trade-off is occurring for theft victims who resist the demands of an assailant. On the one hand, the risk of losing property or cash through theft is decreased (Hindelang et al., 1978: 86-88). On the other hand, the risk of bodily injury to the victim is increased.

The next situational characteristic to be examined in relation to injury is whether the offender possessed a weapon. This variable is related to the risk of injury for theft victims but bears no relation to injury for nontheft victims. Approximately 30% in the latter category received injury regardless of whether the offender possessed a weapon. However, among theft victims, 32% of the incidents resulted in injury when the offender possessed a weapon compared with only 20% of such incidents when no weapon was possessed by the offender.

It is noteworthy that for each of the situational characteristics thus far examined, a relation is present between the observed characteristic and injury for the theft victimizations, but that no relation is apparent for the nontheft victimizations. Again, it appears that separate analysis of theft- and nontheft-related victimizations reveals relations that otherwise would be obscured.

The last situational characteristic to be examined in relation to injury is the type of weapon employed by the offenders. In those incidents where the victim reported that a weapon was used by the offender, the survey asked if it was a gun, a knife, or something other than a gun or a knife.

Table 2 indicates that type of weapon bears a very strong relation to personal injury for both theft- and nontheft-related incidents. In both categories, incidents that involved offenders armed with a gun resulted in a lower risk of injury than was true for incidents that involved offenders with a knife or a weapon classified as "other."[5] Indeed, the risk of injury was even substantially lower for nontheft victims who encountered an assailant with a gun than for such cases in which the offender did not possess a weapon— 13% compared to 31% (see Table 2). In the theft-related category, there was little difference in the risk of injury between incidents that involved an offender armed with a gun and those that involved an offender without a weapon.

From Table 2, it is also observed that incidents involving an offender who possessed a weapon classified as "other" resulted in the largest risk of injury to the victim. This is true for both theft- and nontheft-related incidents. Fifty-four percent of the theft-related incidents involving a weapon classified as "other" resulted in injury to the victim, as well as 46% of the nontheft-related incidents involving this category of weapon (see Table 2). Clearly, these injury percentages are substantially higher than those observed in any other table.

It is likely that several factors account for these relations between injury and type of weapon. For one thing, guns have the potential of easily inflicting grave harm on the victim. Thus, offenders may be very reluctant to use them. In addition, although the data are not shown in tabular form, theft victims who encounter an offender armed with a gun are less likely to employ self-protective measures than are such victims who encounter offenders who possess either a knife or a weapon classified as "other." The strong relation between injury and victim self-protective measures for theft-related incidents has already been discussed. Finally, it is probable that the risk of injury for incidents involving weapons classified as "other" is quite large because weapons of this nature (e.g., clubs, bottles, and so forth) are often not perceived as lethal. Thus the offender is less reluctant to use the weapon. Indeed, there is some evidence that many theft offenders will not employ less intimidating weapons because they are not as effective in establishing control over the victim (Conklin, 1972: 110).

THE EXTENT OF SERIOUS INJURY

Serious injury is defined as any victim-injury that requires medical attention. After observing what portion of victims require such care, analysis will be undertaken to identify the correlates of serious injury. The same variables that were examined in the previous section shall also be explored in relation to serious injury.

Forty percent of the injuries received in theft-related incidents required medical attention, as well as 35% of the injuries received in nontheft-related incidents. Thus, whereas a substantial minority of the injuries in both categories required medical attention, the majority did not.

From the previous section, it is recalled that 23% of the theft-related incidents resulted in injury to the victim as well as 29% of the nontheft-related incidents. Thus it is possible to calculate the proportion of the total group of victimizations that resulted in serious injury to the victim. Multiplying 9.23 x .40 indicates that only 9.2% of the theft victimizations resulted in serious injury. Using a similar calculation, 10.2% of the nontheft victimizations (0.29 x .35) resulted in serious injury to the victim. Thus, regardless of which category is examined, approximately 1 out of 10 victims received serious injury.

SERIOUS INJURY AND VICTIM CHARACTERISTICS

In the first section, it was observed that age is the only victim characteristic that is related to personal injury. At this point, consideration shall be given to the relation between victim characteristics and serious injury.

The data indicate only a few relatively weak relationships between victim characteristics and serious injury. Whereas black/other victims are somewhat more likely to receive serious injury than are white victims regardless of which type of victimization is examined (i.e., theft or nontheft), the differences between the races are relatively small (5%). Likewise, a small relation is observed between age of theft victims and serious injury. Theft victims under 20 years of age are somewhat less likely to receive serious injury (i.e., require medical attention) than are older theft victims. However there is no relation between age of victim and serious injury for nontheft-related victimizations. Finally, the analysis indicates that the sex of the victim is not related to the risk of serious injury for either theft or nontheft victims.

SERIOUS INJURY AND OFFENDER CHARACTERISTICS

Earlier, it was reported that few offender characteristics bear any meaningful relation to personal injury. The analysis shall now determine whether any relations are observed between these same offender characteristics and serious injury.

The fact that race of offender does not bear any relation to personal injury has been discussed. It is also true that race is not related to the risk of serious injury. Regardless of offense category (i.e., theft- or nontheft-related), the likelihood of serious injury does not vary by the race of the offender.

Turning to the question of the relation between the sex of the offender and serious injury, it should be recalled that male theft offenders are somewhat more likely to inflict injury than are female theft offenders. This is also true for serious injury. Theft victimizations perpetrated by male offenders are somewhat more likely to be serious than are those perpetrated by females. The difference (6%) is not large, however. For the nontheft category, there is even less difference between the proportion of serious injury victimizations perpetrated by males and the proportion perpetrated by females.

The last offender characteristic to be examined is age. In the first section, it was observed that age of offender is related to risk of personal injury. However, the relation between these variables is different for theft-related and nontheft-related incidents. On the one hand, the risk of injury is greater for nontheft-related incidents perpetrated by very young offenders than for such incidents perpetrated by offenders of other ages. On the other hand, the risk of injury is lower for theft-related incidents perpetrated by young offenders than for such incidents perpetrated by offenders of other ages.

The above relation between age of offender and injury changes somewhat when serious injury is examined. Very young nontheft offenders (i.e., 14 years or younger) are slightly less likely to inflict serious injury, not more likely to do so than other nontheft offenders. However, young theft offenders are substantially less likely to inflict serious injury than are other theft offenders. This is similar to the pattern observed for theft incidents in the earlier section.

The relations between offender characteristics and serious injury have been discussed. Interestingly enough, for several offender characteristics, the observed relations are similar whether injury or serious injury is examined. The final section shall analyze the relations between situational characteristics and serious injury.

SERIOUS INJURY
AND SITUATIONAL CHARACTERISTICS

In a previous section, it was observed that several situational characteristics strongly relate to injury for theft-related incidents. It was found that theft victims are substantially more likely to be injured if the victimization involved more than one offender, the victim employed self-protective measures, or the offender possessed a weapon. No relations were observed among these variables and nontheft-related incidents. This section examines the relation between serious injury and these situational characteristics.

The analysis indicates that no relation exists between either the numbers of offenders or victim self-protective measures and serious injury. This is true for both theft- and nontheft-related incidents. Thus it is the case that the earlier relations do not hold when the higher threshold definition of serious injury is employed for these variables.

Interestingly enough, the earlier relation does hold for possession of a weapon by an offender. Theft-victims are much more likely to be seriously injured if the offender possesses a weapon than if no weapon is possessed. Sixteen percent of the former result in serious injury compared with 6% of the latter. Among nontheft victims, there is no relation between serious injury and the possession of a weapon by an offender. Thirteen percent of the nontheft victims who encounter an offender with a weapon receive serious injury compared with 9% of such victims who encounter an offender without a weapon.

Turning to the relation between serious injury and type of weapon possessed by the offender, it is observed that weapons classified as "other" are most likely to result in serious injury and that guns are least likely to result in serious injury. Indeed, the rank ordering of the weapons is the same as was observed in the earlier analysis.

The analysis indicates that the risk of serious injury is far higher for theft victims who encounter an offender with a weapon classified as "other" than for any other category of victims. Twenty-six percent of such victims receive serious injury. The next highest risk of serious injury is incurred by nontheft victims who encounter offenders with a weapon classified as "other." Eighteen percent of these victims receive serious injury. The data strongly suggest that the relatively nonlethal nature of many of the weapons in this category decreases the reluctance of offenders to use them, and thus increases both the risk of injury and the risk of serious injury to the victim.

It has been observed that two situational characteristics are strongly related to the risk of serious injury. For one, theft victimizations involving an offender with a weapon are substantially more likely to result in serious injury than are theft victimizations that involve an offender without a weapon. Second, the type of weapon possessed by the offender is strongly related to the risk of serious injury for both theft- and nontheft-related incidents. It is noteworthy that these relations are observed whether the analysis examines the risk of injury or the risk of serious injury.

SUMMARY

This study examined the nature and extent of injury to victims of personal crimes. In addition, the relationships between injury and the following types of variables have been explored: victim characteristics; offender characteristics; and situational characteristics. Two different criteria of injury were employed in the analysis. What follows is a brief list of the more important findings.

(1) Approximately one-quarter of the victims of personal crimes received some injury, and one-tenth of the victims received serious injury.
(2) Nontheft-related victimizations are somewhat more likely to result in some injury than are nontheft-related victimizations. However, no differences exist between type of victimization and the risk of serious injury.
(3) In general, the number of situational characteristics that show a meaningful relation to personal injury is greater than the number of victim or offender characteristics.
(4) The following situational characteristics are strongly re-

lated to personal injury for nontheft-related victimizations: more than one offender; possession of a weapon by the offender; and the employment of self-protective measures by the victim. However, only the relation between possession of a weapon by the offender and injury remains when the higher threshold definition of serious injury is used.

(5) Among victimizations that involve an offender with a weapon, those that involve offenders with a gun are least likely to result in injury to the victim, and those that involve offenders with a weapon classified as "other" are most likely to result in injury. These differences in the risk of injury by type of weapon hold for both theft- and nontheft-related victimizations. In addition, they are quite large regardless of whether the risk of injury or serious injury is examined.

NOTES

1. Only those personal larcenies in which the offender and the victim had contact are included in the analysis.

2. This category includes blacks as well as members of other minority races.

3. When more than one offender was involved, the age recorded is that of the oldest offender. Also, it should be recognized that the age of the offender was obtained by the victim's perception of the age of the offender and that such perceptions may be inaccurate.

4. Weapons other than guns or knives are classified as "other."

5. It should be remembered that victimization surveys include homicide. The FBI reported that 68% of the homicides that occurred during 1974 were committed with firearms (Kelley, 1974: 15). Thus the finding that the risk of serious injury is least for victimizations in which the offender possessed a gun may be somewhat misleading.

REFERENCES

CONKLIN, J. (1972) Robbery and the Criminal Justice System. Philadelphia: J. B. Lippincott.

GAROFALO, J., and M. J. HINDELANG (1978) An Introduction to the National Crime Survey. Analytic Report SD-VAD-4. Law Enforcement Assistance Administration, National Criminal Justice Information and Statistics Service, Washington, DC: Government Printing Office.

HINDELANG, M. J., M. GOTTFREDSON, and J. GAROFALO (1978) Victims of Personal Crimes: An Empirical Foundation for a Theory of Victimization. Cambridge, MA: Ballinger.

HOCHSTEDLER, E. H. (forthcoming) Personal Victimization of the Elderly in Twenty-Six Cities. Analytic Report SD-VAD-11. Law Enforcement Assistance Administration, National Criminal Justice Information and Statistics Service. Washington, DC: Government Printing Office.

KELLEY, C. M. (1974) Crime in the United States: Uniform Crime Reports for 1974. U.S. Department of Justice, Federal Bureau of Investigation, Washington, DC: Government Printing Office.

Lois G. Veronen
Dean G. Kilpatrick
Medical University of South Carolina
Patricia A. Resick
University of South Dakota

10

TREATING FEAR AND ANXIETY IN RAPE VICTIMS
Implications for the Crimimal Justice System

The reason why the psychological status of the victim, particularly her fears and anxieties, should receive attention at a criminal justice symposium on issues of rape, may not be immediately apparent. Yet the rape victim's psychological state and her emotional reactions have an important effect on the process and outcome of her interactions with all parts of the criminal justice system. For example, the victim's psychological state at the time of police interrogation has a considerable effect on the development of a thorough and comprehensive investigation. A confused, incoherent explanation of the assault may result in a fragmented and incomplete investigation. A victim's ability to assist the prosecuting attorney may affect the attorney's ability to prepare the case. In addition, the victim's performance as a witness at the trial is affected by her psychological state. Therefore, excessive fear and anxiety may

AUTHORS' NOTE: *The research for this paper was funded at the Medical University of South Carolina by the National Center for the Prevention and Control of Rape through the National Institute of Mental Health. The research project, entitled "Treatment of Fear and Anxiety in Victims of Rape" (NIMH Grant No. 1 RO1 MH29602), is a cooperative endeavor of the MUSC Department of Psychiatry and Behavioral Sciences and People Against Rape, Inc., a volunteer rape crisis organization in Charleston, SC.*

have debilitating effects at all stages of the victim's interactions with the criminal justice system.

Unfortunately, a review of existing clinical literature regarding the psychological reactions of rape victims shows that existing research leaves much to be considered. The bulk of this work is anecdotal, based on one of only a few clinical cases (Factor, 1954; Sutherland and Scherl, 1970; Werner, 1972; Symonds, 1976), or on large and unsystematic interviews (Burgess and Holmstrom, 1974; Holmstrom and Burgess, 1978). Methodological weakness in description of the subject population, reporting of data, and the use of nonstandardized data gathering procedures limit the generalizability of these findings. In addition, the research has lacked a conceptual basis to integrate and explain the findings (Kilpatrick, forthcoming).

It is our contention that the rape victim experiences significant fear and anxiety as a result of the sexual assault. These fears begin immediately and may continue for months or even years. It is our theoretical position that rape-related fears are classically conditioned, and that some victim fears may be so severe that treatment is required.

The goals of this paper are three: (1) to present a three part model of fear and the conditioning framework which explains the development of fears and phobias in victims of rape; (2) to describe our current research investigation of responses to rape, entitled "Treatment of Fear and Anxiety in Victims of Rape;" and (3) to present the findings of this investigation which have immediate implications for the criminal justice system.

DEVELOPMENT OF RAPE-RELATED
FEARS AND PHOBIAS

Elsewhere (e.g., Kilpatrick et al., 1977; Kilpatrick et al., 1978; Veronen, 1978; Hughes, a.k.a. Veronen, 1976; Veronen and Kilpatrick, 1977; Veronen and Kilpatrick, forthcoming), we have presented a theoretical model which states that fear and anxiety responses are classically conditioned by rape. A full presentation of this model is beyond the scope of this essay, but important varibles in the model will be briefly discussed.

For most victims rape is a life threatening event. The victim is often overwhelmed by force or threat of force, confined, restricted, or in some way made powerless. A victim's experience of this event as a threat to her life is the unconditioned stimulus which provides the basis for the development of subsequent fears and phobias. This unconditioned stimulus evokes unconditioned responses of terror and extreme anxiety. Stimuli paired or associated with the unconditioned stimulus can also elicit anxiety and fear. These conditioned stimuli, such as persons, situations, and events present at the time of the terror-inducing rape, can produce subsequent fear. The classical conditioning literature also predicts that those fears may generalize: Persons, situations, or events which are similar to the initial ones may also elicit fear from the victim. Additionally, repeated exposure or threat of exposure to the life threatening trauma will increase the magnitude of the fear. Finally, the greater the number of rape-related stimuli present, the more intense the fear reaction will be.

Anxiety and fear are best understood as theoretical constructs. A useful model for conceptualizing the anxiety and fear may be expressed in one or more of three channels: physiological, cognitive, and behavioral. Physiological manifestations of fear are physiological changes such as increases in heart rate, shortness of breath, queasy or nauseous stomach, and increased sweating of the palms. Cognitive manifestations of fear may be frightening images, thoughts, or flashbacks. Instrumental behavior manifestations of fear and anxiety may be avoidance of the feared situation, an attempt to escape from a fear-inducing situation, freezing, or fighting. Obviously, there is an interplay of these three channels in a victim's expressions of fear, but it is important to remember that fear may occur in all, some, or none of the three channels.

TREATMENT OF FEAR:
RESEARCH INVESTIGATION

Our investigation is an attempt to better understand the acquisition of fear and anxiety among victims of rape. It has two parts: (1) an assessment of victim psychological reactions over a 1-year period; and (2) a treatment efficacy study.

In the assessment of victim reactions, a group of recent rape victims and a group of comparison subjects, matched for age, race, and residential neighborhood, were tested on 5 occasions: (1) 6 to 10 days postrape; (2) 1 month postrape; (3) 3 months postrape; (4) 6 months postrape; and (5) 1 year postrape. The assessment measures were objective, standardized measures of fear, anxiety, moods, psychological complaints, self-esteem, and self-concept. In addition, a structured clinical interview was conducted by a psychologist during three of the assessment sessions. This study is the first to assess victims longitudinally, to use standardized, reliable and valid assessment instruments, and to compare victims with an appropriate group of nonraped women.

In the treatment study, victims of rape who experienced significant fear and anxiety at three months postrape or later, selected one of three treatment options: stress inoculation, systematic desensitization, or peer counseling. The design for this study was a combination of single case methodology and group methodology. Each victim identified three target behaviors or situations where they experienced excessive fear. Psychophysiological indices of skin conductance and heart rate, as well as self-report fear thermometer ratings, were taken on each target behavior prior to, after treatment for target behavior one and two, at the end of treatment, and at the end of the three-month follow-up. Group outcome measures, using standard psychological tests, allowed a comparison of the three treatment approaches. These measures were administered pre- and posttreatment, and at the three-month follow-up.

Results of the victim assessment research suggest that victims are severely traumatized by rape. At the 6-10 day assessment and throughout the one-month assessment, the victim group was significantly impaired on many of the psychological measures in contrast to the comparison group. Preliminary data suggest that rape immediately precipitates severe self-rated mood disturbance and disorganization of behavior. At the three-month follow-up, however, the victim population appeared to have generally regained its psychological equilibrium. The global indices of pathology and disruption dissipated. Remaining elevations in test scores were focalized in the area of fear and anxiety; elevated scores such as suspiciousness and anxiety, as well as specific fear survey scores, support the notion that excessive fear and anxiety remain, and that specific fears and anxieties are rape-related.

In the interest of discussing the data most relevant to the criminal justice system, let us turn to victim fear reactions at the time of the rape and after. Lang's (1969) tripartite model of fear suggested that victims could manifest fear in any of three channels. Often, both the number of feared situations and intensity of fears decrease, so it is important to assess fears at several postrape intervals to determine whether some indices of fear would remain stable.

As part of our investigation, a structured interview was conducted by a psychologist requesting victims to identify symptoms they experienced during the rape, and in the 2-3 hour postrape period. The victims were also asked to rate the severity of the symptoms. Preliminary analysis of the findings from the interviews of the 25 victims, presented in Table 1, suggests that the victims experienced profound cognitive and psychological symptoms of anxiety during the rape. With respect to cognitive symptoms of anxiety the victims reported feeling worried (96%), scared (96%), terrified (92%), confused (92%), exhausted (52%), and had racing thoughts (80%) and ruminated about the rape (64%). Symptoms of physiological anxiety included shaking or trembling (96%), racing heart (84%), pain (72%), rapid breathing (64%), tight muscles (68%), and numbness (60%).

TABLE 1
Percentage of Victims Experiencing Cognitive and Physiological
Symptoms During the Rape and 2-3 Hours Postrape

Symptom	During Rape	2-3 Hours Postrape
Cognitive Symptoms:		
Anger	80%	80%
Ashamed—Humiliated	72%	80%
Confused	92%	80%
Depressed	48%	84%
Exhausted	52%	96%
Feelings of unreality	64%	60%
Guilty	48%	52%
Helpless	88%	76%
Jumpy—restless	NA	88%
Racing thoughts	80%	80%
Ruminating	64%	68%
Scared	96%	88%
Terrified	92%	80%
Withdrawn	24%	76%
Worried	96%	96%
Physiological Symptoms:		
Dry mouth	44%	52%
Felt physically relaxed	4%	12%
Headache	16%	60%
Heart racing	84%	48%
Numbness	60%	48%
Pain	72%	68%
Rapid breathing	64%	44%
Shaking or trembling	96%	96%
Tight muscles	68%	68%

Victims remained fearful and anxious during the 2 or 3-hour postrape period. They experienced cognitive symptoms of worry (96%), exhausion (96%), jumpy-restlessness (88%), fright (88%), confusion (80%), racing throughts (80%), and terror (80%). Frequently experienced symptoms of physiological anxiety included shaking or trembling (96%), pain (68%), tight muscles (68%), headache (60%), and dry mouth (52%). It is important to note that many of the cognitive symptoms of anxiety were actually *greater* during the post-rape period.

These data, which document the emotional distress experienced by victims 2 or 3 hours after the rape, suggest the advisability of adjusting the timing of the interview conducted by the investigating officer. In Charleston, as well as many other places, this interview is conducted before or immediately after the evidentiary exam at the county emergency room. Our data suggest that this interview could be more efficiently conducted after the intense reactions of the victim abated. Perhaps the initial investigation could gather only information useful in identifying the suspect, leaving questioning on other issues for a later interrogation.

Our research also addressed the issue of testifying in court. In past years, the victim's treatment in court has aroused considerable attention. Holmstrom and Burgess (1978) recently concluded that the court experience precipitated as much of a psychological crisis for the rape victim as the rape itself. Others suggest that a rape victim is twice victimized—by the sexual assault and by her experience in court (Borgida and Oksner, 1978).

As other aspects of victim reaction research have been clouded by emotionalism and suffered from lack of systematically collected data, so it is with a victim's court testimony. Information gathered from the unstructured interviews of Holmstrom and Burgess (1978) indicates that victims fear testifying in court but, unfortunately, these fears were not compared with those of nonraped women. Research conducted as part of our study bears directly on the issue of testifying in court. Recent rape victims and their comparison group completed the Modified Fear Survey five times during a one-year period as part of the larger assessment. The Modified Fear Survey (Veronen and Kilpatrick, 1977) includes some commonly feared items and rape-related situations. Participants are instructed to rate items according to the degree of subjective disturbance produced by the item on a five-point scale from "not at all" to "very much" disturbing. A more complete report of this research is presented elsewhere (Kilpatrick et al., 1978). Since this research has not been completed, not all participants have completed all assessment sessions. Thirty victims were assessed at the first session, and 22 victims have completed the 6-month assessment. Thity-one comparison group nonvictims have been assessed at the first session, and 18 have completed the 6-month assessment. A measure of total fearfulness indicated that victims were significantly more fearful than comparison nonvictims at each of the four assessments. In addition, overall scores indicated that victims became less fearful during the 3 months following the rape. At the 6-month assessment, however, there was a tendency for total fearfulness scores of the victims to increase somewhat. Our clinical judgment suggests that, at three months postrape, there is a strong tendency for victims to deny and ignore disturbances in mood and alterations of behavior; whereas, by the time of the 6-month session, the victim accurately reports her degree of disturbance.

In addition to the total score computations discussed above, discrepancy scores were computed for each item of the Modified Fear Survey by subtracting the mean comparison group from the mean victim group scores. Represented in Table 2 are the 10 items at each of the four assessment sessions which had the greatest discrepancy between victims and comparison subjects.

At the 6 to 10-day postrape assessment, testifying in court occupied a relatively high position, indicating that victims feared testifying in court while nonvictims did not. The only items producing greater discrepancy scores at this assessment were being alone, people behind you, a man's penis, and venereal disease. The nature of these feared items strongly supports a classical conditioning model for the development of rape-related fears. At the 1-month postrape period, testifying in court remained highly provocative of fear, but at the 3-month and 6-month postrape periods, fear of testifying in court had abated and was no longer among the top ten fears. But this finding may be somewhat misleading. It is possible that those victims whose cases were dropped by the police, whose assailants were not apprehended, or whose cases were already tried, were those whose fear had dissipated. We are investigating this hypothesis. Another interesting finding is that speaking in public at the 3-month and talking to police at the 6-month postrape periods were rated as highly fear-inducing.

That court testimony produces fear and anxiety for victims of rape is understandable, given the constellation of fear-evoking cues. Classical conditioning theory predicts that the intensity of a subsequent fear response will be related to the nature and number of stimuli or cues present. During the court proceedings, the victim is required to present a verbal report, a re-enactment, of the assault. In addition to the cognitive cues produced by this testimony, the presence of the assailant is an additional stimulus which intensifies her fear response.

SUMMARY AND IMPLICATIONS

Thus far, we have presented a theoretical model which predicts the development of fear responses following a rape. We have produced empirical data in support of this model which shows that victims are extremely anxious during the rape and in the hours which follow. Since high levels of anxiety have a disruptive influence on normal cognitive and intellectual functioning, we have demonstrated that the rape victim may have great difficulty in: (a) perceiving and remembering details of the rape; and (b) reporting these details to the authorities during the interrogation. We have shown that victims are more fearful than nonvictims, that fears are rape-related, that fears persist, and that potential interactions with the criminal justice system, such as talking with police and testifying in court, produce great fear.

What are the implications of these findings? First, police should not expect victims to give completely accurate statements a few hours after the rape. As has been suggested previously, delaying complete interrogation until the victim's anxiety has diminished would be humane and produce more complete, accurate information as well. A related point is that victims can be expected to remember more as their anxiety lessens. Therefore, it is inappropriate to

TABLE 2
Modified Fear Survey (MFS) Items with Greatest Discrepancy
Scores Between Victim and Comparison Subjects by Session

6-10 Days Postrape

1. Being alone
2. People behind you
3. Man's penis
4. Venereal disease
5. Testifying in court
6. Being in a strange place
7. Crowds
8. Anal intercourse
9. Darkness
10. Blind dates

1 Month Postrape

1. Darkness
2. Being alone
3. Strangers
4. People behind you
5. Testifying in court
6. Walking on a dimly lit street
7. Door slamming
8. Being in a strange place
9. Venereal disease
10. Being awakened at night

3 Months Postrape

1. Being alone
2. Strangers
3. People talking about you
4. Being watched working
5. Going out with new people
6. Angry people
7. Sudden noises
8. Being criticized
9. Insane people
10. Speaking in public

6 Months Postrape

1. Being alone
2. Talking to police
3. Crowds
4. Strangers
5. Being awakened at night
6. Blind dates
7. Insane people
8. Going out with new people
9. Sudden noises
10. People behind you

impugn the victim's veracity because of the predictable changes in information she gives the police.

Second, the extent to which victims are disturbed by potential court appearances has implications for legal reform and for other policies as well. Some rape crisis centers have discontinued the practice of encouraging victims to prosecute. They concluded that the humiliation and degradation were not worth the opportunity for prosecution.

Elsewhere, reformed rape legislation has made testifying less anxiety producing for the victim. According to Borgida and Oskner (1978), 40 states have rape shield reform statutes which limit, to varying degrees, the admissibility of the victim's prior sexual history with persons other than the defendant.

A third implication is that special treatment of extreme fears may be indicated. Of particular relevance in dealing with court-related fear and anxiety is one of the treatment options which we are investigating as part of our ongoing research. Stress Inoculation Training (SIT) is a cognitive behavioral treatment (Meichenbaum, 1977) for fear and anxiety. This approach recognizes that fear and anxiety are unavoidably a part of everyday life. The first phase of treatment involves offering the victim an explanatory scheme for her reactions to the recent rape, the nature and origin of her present fears, and how fears are experienced in each of the three channels. The next portion of treatment is organized around the instruction and rehearsal of coping skills to deal with the indices or symptoms of fear which occur in each of the three channels. The victim applies these coping skills to manage lesser fears and stressors, thereby inoculating herself against being overwhelmed by a major stressor. In the final phase of treatment, the victim confronts the significant fears which she has identified. This treatment has specific skills to deal with many of the cognitive fear symptoms, such as rumination and negative self-devaluations, which often affect the victim facing a court appearance.

Finally, there are steps short of professional treatment which could reduce court-related fear and anxiety. Lack of information about procedures contributes to anxiety maintenance; simply providing information about her case would reduce the fear of the unknown. Similarly, proper pretrial perparation, including the appropriate use of behavioral rehearsal and role-playing techniques, would probably reduce anxiety, thereby assisting the state's case by increasing the victim's ability to present her story effectively.

REFERENCES

BORGIDA, E., and P. OKSNER (1978) "Perception of rape victims: the impact of evidentiary reform." Presented at the annual meeting of the American Psychological Association, Toronto, Canada.

BURGESS, A. W., and L. L. HOLMSTROM (1974) Rape: Victims of Crisis. Bowie, MD: Robert J. Bradly.

FACTOR, M. (1954) "A woman's psychological reaction to attempted rape." Psychoanalytic Q. 23: 243-244.

HOLMSTROM, L. L. and A. W. BURGESS (1978) The Victim of Rape: Institutional Reactions. New York: John Wiley.

HUGHES, a.k.a. L. J. VERONEN (1976) "Fear response of rape victims." Presented at the 12th Annual Convention of the Southeastern Psychological Association, New Orleans.

KILPATRICK, D. G. (forthcoming) "The scientific study of rape: a clinical research perspective," in R. Green and J. Wiener (eds.) Methodology in Sex Research. Washington, DC: Government Printing Office.

———, C. L. BEST, and L. J. VERONEN (1978) "The adolescent rape victim: psychological responses to sexual assault and treatment approaches," in A. K. Kreutner and D. R. Hollingsworth (eds.) Adolescent Obstetrics and Gynecology. Chicago: Year Book Medical Publishers.

KILPATRICK, D. G., L. J. VERONEN, and P. A. RESICK (1978) "The aftermath of rape: changing patterns of fear." Presented at the 12th Annual Convention of the Association for Advancement of Behavior Therapy, Chicago.

———, L. J. VERONEN, and P. A. RESICK (1977) "Responses to rape: behavioral perspectives and treatment approaches." Scandinavian J. of Behavior Therapy 6: 85.

LANG, P. J. (1969) "The mechanics of desensitization and laboratory studies of human fear," in C. M. Franks (ed.) Assessment and Status of the Behavioral Therapies and Associated Developments. New York: McGraw Hill.

MEICHENBAUM, D. (1977) Cognitive-Behavior Modification: An Integrative Approach. New York: Plenum Press.

SUTHERLAND, S., and D. SCHERL (1970) "Patterns of response among victims of rape." Amer. J. of Orthopsychiatry 40: 503-511.

SYMONDS, M. (1976) "The rape victim: psychological patterns of response." Amer. J. of Psychoanalysis 36: 27-34.

VERONEN, L. J. (1977) "Fear response of rape victims." Ph.D. Dissertation, North Texas State University.

——— (forthcoming) "Self-reported fears of rape victims: a preliminary investigation." Behavior Modification.

——— and D. G. KILPATRICK (1977) "Contiditioned fear and anxiety in victims of rape." Presented at the 11th Annual Convention of the Association for Advancement of Behavior Therapy, Atlanta.

WERNER, A. (1972) "Rape: interruption of the therapeutic process of external stress." Psychotherapy: Theory, Research, and Practice 9: 249-351.

ABOUT THE AUTHORS

WILLIAM E. BERG is Associate Professor in the School of Social Welfare at the University of Wisconsin-Milwaukee, and a member of the Graduate Faculty in the Criminal Justice Program.

MARK BLUMBERG is Research Assistant at the Criminal Justice Research Center and a doctoral student in the School of Criminal Justice at SUNY, Albany.

DAVID L. DECKER is currently Associate Professor of Sociology at California State College, San Bernardino.

EDNA EREZ is presently an Assistant Professor of Criminal Justice at the University of Baltimore.

SIMON HAKIM is Assistant Professor of Economics at Temple University.

JOHN R. HEPBURN is Associate Professor of the Administration of Justice, Pennsylvania State University.

ROBERT JOHNSON is currently Associate Professor of Justice at the American University, Washington, D.C.

DEAN G. KILPATRICK is Associate Professor in the Department of Psychiatry and Behavioral Sciences, Medical University of South Carolina.

DANIEL J. MONTI is Assistant Professor of Sociology at the University of Missouri at St. Louis.

JAMES F. NELSON is a Research Associate with the Criminal Justice Research Center, and Adjunct Professor of Sociology, SUNY, Albany.

ROBERT M. O'BRIEN is Associate Professor of Sociology at California State College, San Bernardino.

WILLIAM H. PARSONAGE is Associate Professor of Administration of Justice in the College of Human Development, The Pennsylvania State University, and Faculty Associate to the Dean for Commonwealth Campuses and Continuing Education.

CARL E. POPE is Associate Professor of Criminal Justice at the University of Wisconsin-Milwaukee.

PATRICIA A. RESICK is Assistant Professor in the Department of Psychology, University of South Dakota.

DAVID SHICHOR is currently Associate Professor of Sociology at California State College, San Bernardino.

SAMUEL D. SMITHYMAN is on the staff at the Human Sciences Center, Beverly Hills, California.

LOIS J. VERONEN is Assistant Professor in the Department of Psychiatry and Behavioral Sciences, Medical University of South Carolina.

VERNETTA D. YOUNG is an Instructor in the School of Justice at the American University, Washington, D.C.